An African
Living with Depression
in America

Stephen Kwame

iUniverse books may be ordered through booksellers or by contacting:

iUniverse
1663 Liberty Drive
Bloomington, IN 47403
www.iuniverse.com
1-800-Authors (1-800-288-4677)

Because of the dynamic nature of the Internet, any Web addresses or links contained in this book may have changed since publication and may no longer be valid. The views expressed in this work are solely those of the author and do not necessarily reflect the views of the publisher, and the publisher hereby disclaims any responsibility for them.

ISBN: 978-1-4502-2016-3 (sc)
ISBN: 978-1-4502-2015-6 (e)

Print information available on the last page.

iUniverse rev. date: 03/24/2017

This book is dedicated to the Memory of Mr. Aga and also to Dr. and Mrs. Halvorson and Mama, and the great Dr. Stephen Chabot and all workers of Gateway, Bacon Street, Pawtucket, RI, USA.

Other than Mr. Aga, Dr. and Mrs. Loren Halvorson, Dr. Stephen Chabot and the Africans in the book, all names are fictitious and only in the imagination of the author

About the Author

Stephen Kwame is a graduate of Gustavus Adolphus College, St. Peter, Minnesota in 1979 with degrees in Biology and Classics. He graduated from the Ohio State University, Columbus, Ohio with an M. A. in Black Studies in 1982.

Stephen taught at T.I. Ahmadiyya Secondary School for ten years in Kumasi, Ghana. Upon return to the United States, Stephen worked with the Fortune 500 High Technology Company, Texas Instruments in Attleboro, Massachusetts for ten years. He has been an adjunct professor at Rhode Island College for sixteen years, teaching in the African-American Studies program.

Stephen is married with three children, two of whom are in college at Rhode Island College and the University of Rhode Island. He has also taught at the Providence School District as an L.T.S.P. for the past four years. Stephen has an avid love for students and he surely believes that teaching is his calling.

His hobbies include reading and writing, watching the New England Patriots win football games, editing students' writing at no cost, and enjoying a mirthful laugh with his best friend of 16 years, Silas Obadiah (a Nigerian graduate from Brown University).

Introduction

I have always wanted to write about my experiences as a person with depression in America because, in the U.S., being an African, black and "insane," my situation was grim indeed. Yet, with all these attributes never have I encountered racism or discrimination because of my nationality, color or disability in this country where these things abound.

I have been blessed with excellent and very kind-hearted people like Mr. Aga and his daughter Marilyn Roesler (my American sister), Dr. Loren Halvorson and his wife Ruth of Arc Retreat Center in Stanchfield, Minnesota, Dr. and Mrs. Freiert (Classics Department, Gustavus Adolphus 1975-79), and the great Dr. Stephen Chabot (a graduate of Brown University Medical School and my psychiatrist who has taken care of me for about 20 years without charging me a penny, imagine that!), amazing Mama, Kalala, Nellie, and the awesome Silas Obadiah.

Unfortunately, everywhere in the world, mental illness is a basis for ridicule, shame and crime. Yes, there is the criminally insane, but most mentally sick people live under the umbrella of shame and worthlessness. Even in America, the most powerful nation in the world, most of the mentally sick, I know, get their disability insurance and retreat into a life of nothingness and dependence on medication. Don't count me out because I have also taken medication daily for thirty-five years and I don't know why God hasn't called me as He has done Anna Nicole Smith and Michael Jackson (a great waste of beauty and legendary talent). I have taken sixteen pills daily for thirty-five years.

Believe it or not, it is some of these same mentally sick people who have contributed hugely to creativity and science in the world, like Lord Byron, Tchaikovsky, Dostoevsky, Van Gogh, Carl Jung, and even, perhaps, Hemingway (who was so dissatisfied with the world that he killed himself). Also, there are the great minds in science like Charles Darwin and Isaac

Newton. These maestros' contributions to the world are unparalleled. Maybe scientists should isolate the gene that causes depression with its concomitant creativity.

Cleverly, some criminals, when they have committed heinous crimes, want to be identified with mental illness, and this is brought up by defense lawyers. This destroys the unfortunate weight or yoke hanging around the mentally sick peoples' necks and ignominy of the illness.

Ridiculous and derogatory expressions like, "Are you nuts?" "Have you lost your bearings?" "He is cuckoo!" "He is crazy?" "He is loony." "You've gone bananas," don't help the mentally sick one bit.

It is my hope that people will read my small book with objectivity and a lot of hope and faith in God; the only one who gives succor to everyone.

Everybody has a yoke, be it mental illness, Lupus, Multiple Sclerosis, Cancer, Heart Disease, Impotence, Obesity, Childlessness, Dwarfism, Epilepsy, Asthma and so on and on. I wouldn't trade my condition for anything else.

As my great friend, Silas Obadiah, always says: Life is worth living when the healthy help the sick, the rich help the poor, and the strong help the weak. Life is not about one person accumulating millions or billions of dollars when others are homeless and sleeping under bridges. After all, we all eat the same rice, potatoes, burgers, sausage, bananas, cauliflower, or Brussels sprouts. The rich man or woman cannot say, "I have billions so my rice should be gold and my water should be mercury or my meat should be diamond." Air, water and food are what make us all human, so if you have them, please share, as I have always done.

It is my hope that this book will inspire more sympathy, respect, and dignity for those with my medical condition. They too are humans who love all and wish to be loved by all. I also hope that the book will encourage those with my condition to be strong in adversity, to always remember as I did, that they are an inseparable part of the human family and should endeavor to live fully, love abundantly, have friends and raise families. These are the sustaining things I did during my tough struggle. I love the fact that God helped me to remain steadfast and always hopeful for better days.

I have no regrets at all. Indeed, the same divine force is ever present and eager to uplift, sustain and, at times, heal you when all else seem bleak and hopeless. Great thanks to God for sustaining me in my 35 year struggle with this condition and for helping me not to commit a minor infringement or crime ever.

Stephen Kwame

Contents

Chapter I

First Days in College

Of all the things I have lost, my mind is the one I miss the most. I have lost this mind about twenty times, and every time I lost it, I found it back to live an unprecedented and happy life full of hope and faith in God. It all began on a college campus in the Fall of 1974 in Minnesota.

Some leaves adjusted to the force of gravity, fell from their sustaining branches, and danced solemnly to Mother Earth to join others on the ground which had suffered the same fate. There was a light breeze, of course, and there was a rustling of the leaves on the ground. The weather was heavenly. It was Indian summer in Minnesota. It was autumn, and as the Americans call it, it was fall in Minnesota. The town was St. Peter, and like many close-knit towns in Minnesota, it was full of sobriety. Yet, unlike many small towns in Minnesota, there was no lake seen, quite uncharacteristic of this state which nature and the glacier age had endowed with, as the natives would say, "ten thousand lakes."

Gustavus Adolphus College was located on top of a valley. It was actually solitary, yet vibrant with academic life. The carpet of grass in front of the entrance was a carefully mowed riot of green. A cluster of pine trees and fir whistled their happiness at the welcome breeze, and birch, maple and elm stood with dignity and were well arranged. The road climbed steadily up and my American father's Brougham, with all the comfort a man could have in a car, rode up without a single sigh. Yes, comfortable America indeed! I looked out and saw a bright red cardinal flutter its majesty through the pines. In color contrast, a dull, brown robin flew quickly after a large monarch butterfly with orange-brown wings. The whole setting was elegant and pulsating with life.

Father stopped some blondish girls and asked directions in a magnificent bass, contrasting with the almost soprano voices of the girls. The girls pointed to a huge, red-brick building, and soon, we were in front of Co-ed Hall.

I had, finally, made it to an American college. It was the first day of my freshman year, and I was overawed by the dignity and serenity of the place, small as I had seen. I was anxious to get around. After my graying father helped me with my belongings and we were finally in my room, third floor co-ed, I gave a big sigh of relief and thanked my father graciously. He had been giving me a whole string of advice of do's and don'ts in an American college. My American father was not an ordinary man. He had not gone to college but had made it as a very important man in the town of Alexandria. He owned a radio station, KXRA, in the town. I had known this man before in 1972 and up until today, his magnificent generosity and great altruism had remained without question. In fact, I had lived with him for only six months as an American Field Service (A.F.S.) exchange student in the academic year of 1971-72. So you see, this was not my first time of coming to the United States. This year was 1974. I will tell you more about the years 1971-72 and this man later, but let us get back to this serene setting of Gustavus Adolphus, which as I look back was bringing adversity. This place, instantly, filled me with self-confidence so unparalleled in my life that I was already running into the dangerous apogee of delusion. I had come to G.A.C. (short for Gustavus Adolphus College) as a promising pre-medical student. I told myself that I had to get all A's in all my courses. Somehow, unknowingly, I had started out, deluded by the serenity of the setting, that I was in a singular class of my own, quite oblivious of my very humble beginnings, parents, and home in my ever-loving mother Ghana.

As soon as I entered my section of Co-ed Hall, I asserted myself and greeted with a warm and confident, "Hi, guys." My hall mates responded in unison. The only black guy there was Eric, an African-American from California. He was a husky, handsome guy sporting a big Afro. He was bowlegged, but not enough to disagree with his handsomeness. He was handsome because nature had generously endowed him with hairs all over the body. He was bare-chested, and the hair on his chest made him look more handsome according to the girls. He was very muscular, and I later learned that the golden-haired girls were very impressed by those muscles.

These excellent attributes gave the girls with pear-shaped breasts what they fantasized about. He greeted me with, "What's happening?"

I didn't know how to respond to this strange greeting for he was only about the only real African-American I had met yet. You know, most parts of small town Minnesota are lily white.

"Nothing is happening, why?" was my response.

"Come on, brother. Welcome, man."

"Thank you."

I later learned that with the African-American, every black man was a "brother." The whites never called themselves brother.

Eric soon realized that I wasn't a real brother, but only a color brother. I spoke with an accent.

"You from Africa?"

"Yes."

"Oh, Tarzan brother, c'mon have a seat, man."

He gave me a chair and told me about G.A.C. He had just finished his sophomore year, and he was our hall captain. After a few moments with Eric, I saw that he was not ordinary, although I was a bit disappointed, sometimes, when I couldn't get all his so-called Black English vernacular. Sometimes, he spoke Ebonics. Yes, the whites said the blacks spoke vernacular English and they spoke Midwestern standard English. I didn't know where to put my English, but Eric soon realized that I spoke crisp and correct English in spite of my accent. Eric stood up a while, and then sat down. He made gestures with his hands, always touching me with his forefinger, and as he talked, added "man" to every sentence. Later, he would strut, with a swagger and a gait only known to the modern black American man who is finding more ways to assert his pride and confidence in a society in which he is often called a second-class citizen.

As Eric was talking excitedly and gesticulating with his hands, and I was listening with gleeful attention, a youthful red-haired guy entered the hall, followed by his parents and brothers and sisters. He greeted us with, "Hi, guys," then asked, "Please where is Room 303?"

"Room 303, you said?" I asked.

"Yes."

"That's my room, too."

"Oh, we are roommates then. I am Mark. What's yours?"

"Kwame."

"What?!"

"I said, 'Kwame.'"

"How do you spell it?"

"C'mon, Kwame is easy enough to pronounce. You mean you haven't heard about Kwame Nkrumah before?"

"Who is he?"

I raised my eyes and gave up. Everybody knows Kwame Nkrumah, except American children who know next to nothing about the rest of the world. America is the world.

I said my name again and Mark practiced saying it a few times and registered it. I stood up and excused myself from Eric and led Mark past his family to Room 303. In the room, Mark introduced me to his mom and dad, as his brothers and sisters listened. They all said, "Nice to meet you," and smiled. I noticed that they were not disappointed in me, a black boy, as their son's roommate. I wasn't surprised, because a good many Minnesotans are more tolerant of blacks and foreigners as I had discovered in the years of 1971 and 1972.

As we made one another's acquaintance, I immediately discerned that the Halvorson family was a very wonderful, humane family more inclined to goodness than to the evil of the racial bigotry and discrimination. For one thing, Dr. Halvorson was a Lutheran pastor who taught at Luther Seminary in St. Paul, the state capital of Minnesota. Dr. Halvorson was also red haired with a thinning hairline. He actually had a bald pate, but concealed in a nice way by hairs from the sides of his temple. He was streaked with some grey hair, although I could see he was relatively younger than my American father. He wore glasses and also an elaborate beauteous smile. I discovered he spoke and wrote German well.

On his right was Paul, his eldest son, who was already a sophomore at Augsburg College in Minneapolis. He also had his father's strong and dominant red-hair genes. He was taller than Mark and a bit heavier. Next to him was Mrs. Halvorson. I heard Dr. Halvorson call her Ruth, so it registered, obviously, as her name. She was dark-haired and curly. She had a dignified, pious aura around her and her voice was distinct and mellow. I saw two compassionate eyes, also softly set, and dark. Their two daughters stood leaning by Mark's bed. Mary was a hair taller than Becky. They were both appealing to the visual senses but I, in particular, liked the looks of Becky. Mary had sandy, long hair and Becky had long, dark hair that curled at the bottom. They were both young and in high school. Becky's cheeks were flushed. I thought she was blushing or had rouge on but later I found that she had naturally rosy cheeks. Mary was serious but Becky, like her father, was wearing a Mona Lisa smile. Last of the children was Joel. He had the legs of a runner. His hair, also sandy colored, had some locks at the forehead which he unconsciously, once in a while, brushed back with his right fingers. Mark was the most rustic of the lot in terms of appearance. I could see that he was more comical than the rest, given to subtle jokes, and also had a warm smile. I saw immediate mutual friendship and pleasant acquaintanships take root there and then.

It was getting late so Mark and I saw his family off in their new Volvo station wagon, which they bought in Sweden. They were there.

We engaged each other in inquisitive and probing conversation and headed towards the cafeteria, climbed the stairs, and showed our identification cards to the lady dressed in white with white shoes. The school matron had welcomed us with steak and baked potatoes with superfluous butter. As we took our full trays and entered the main cafeteria, the place took an altogether new and different aspect. Immediately, I noticed that a scarce population of blacks was seated by themselves at the back of one corner. Immediately, I thought the place was segregated because, here too, the blacks were obviously a paltry minority and no white person was among them. I later discovered that it was just a matter of their own choice because they felt more comfortable with members of their own color. I broke this uncomfortable rule, in my view, and sat with Mark and some other white boys and girls. We ate the victuals with relish, punctuated, here and there, with clanging cutlery and laughter. After the supper, Mark took me downstairs to the game room where there was a ping-pong table. It was apparent that freshman Mark knew the place better than myself. When I asked him how he was doing so well taking me around, he laughed and said, "Kwame, you came all the way from Africa. I just live in St. Paul, and we have driven here several times to visit since my admission."

"Well, that explains it," I said.

When we returned to Co-ed, we went to the basement and sat in the plush, blue shaggy-carpeted sitting room for students and watched a color television until late. Mark bought himself and myself some candy and we went upstairs to bed. It was an agreeable first day, and I thought I had learned a lot. However, there was something sinister about my other hall mates who delighted in smoking pipes (I wonder what was in the pipes), playing their stereos very loudly, and once in a while, eating what they called chili from cans, and some crackers.

The following day was Sunday. G.A.C. is a Lutheran college and has a chapel well architected in triangular shapes right in the middle of the campus. Obviously, Mark wanted to introduce me to Martin Luther's church as soon as he could, but I declined to go. Services were held every Sunday and every weekday morning. I was a staunch Catholic and wanted to remain so. I gathered that a Catholic priest from town said mass on Saturday evenings so I had missed the Caltholic mass. I decided to join Eric and go to church for the first time with my black brothers and sisters. I was surprised by their emotion-filled service full of shouts of "Jesus, Amen, Amen, Jesus, and Praise the Lord." It was an uncomfortable change from the sober Catholic mass which I was much used to. I could not sit still. I didn't know their songs. It seemed some of them were in a trance speaking some gibberish. I didn't understand it. Some people were even crying out of emotion. There was no priest or pastor and the students took turns to go to the pulpit to preach.

After what seemed like an eternal time of this, a request came for any newcomer, who wanted to, to introduce himself and give a small talk. I stood up with overconfidence and went to the pulpit to introduce myself. The impromptu sermon I gave was later described as deep by one of the girls. I didn't quite know what to make of this. When, finally, the service came to an end, I went straight to Eric, who was, as usual, busily talking and gesticulating to his friends. His voice was a steady baritone but occasionally, in order to make a point, a high-pitched falsetto will intervene.

"Ki-w-a-me," he said. "How did you like our service?" touching me on the shoulder.

"I was scared."

"Really," he shouted. "C'mon, Kiwame, you mean you never went to service before?"

"Yes, but not this one."

"This is what I call a Black Baptist service. You liked it, din't ya, man?"

"This is the first time I have seen so much emotion expressed in one service."

"C'mon, don't think we were nuts in there. That's the best way to worship. Ain't it, Dick?"

"You better believe it," Dick said and cackled. As we walked on and talked, I took a small inventory of myself in two days. I noticed that I had been unduly bold and overconfident. The Baptist worship accentuated it in some way. I felt scared a bit because I was usually not emotional.

Chapter II

First Encounter with Depression

Monday was for registration of classes and general acquaintance with the school. I registered four classes with the help of my counselor. I had taken freshman biology, chemistry, physics and French and other physical education courses for the fall semester. I went back to the dormitory and saw Mark who had finished with his registration a while back.

"What courses are you taking, Kwam?"

"Biology, chemistry, physics, and French."

"Wow, you have such a load, Kwam."

"Oh, I can handle it, don't worry," I said confidently again and chortled mirthfully.

"Do you know all your classrooms yet?"

"They are on my registration form, but I don't exactly know where they are. Where is the auditorium? I have biology there."

"I'll show you, c'mon, let's go."

Mark took me around to all the classrooms that were not too distant from one another. Some of them were even in the same building. I was impressed about Nobel Auditorium. It had several pictures of Nobel prize winners on the walls, and a rather huge and long pedulum was swinging nonchalantly in the center of the building.

"Why is this place called Nobel Auditorium and why these pictures, Mark?"

"I have heard that G.A.C. holds a Nobel Conference every year and invites several Nobel prize winners to the school. They say it's a real celebration." Mark added.

"I am looking forward to meeting these minds of the world. In fact, I have read about them in Irving Wallace's book, The Prize. I really admire these people."

"You will get your chance to meet them," Mark said.

The conversation switched from Nobel prize winners to sports.

"What sports do you play?" Mark asked.

"I was once a track star in high school. As a matter of fact, I was able to make it to the Minnesota State Meet in 1972. You know, I won the regionals in the 440 yards. I still have my medals, and I will show them to you when we get back to our room. Remind me."

I wasn't very good in soccer at home, but when I heard that the Americans were worse players, I decided to show them a few tricks or two. In the two weeks that followed, soccer became my biggest letdown.

Classes started briskly. I carried my books which I had gotten from the Book Mark and walked to my classes. I got lost a few times and had to ask directions. I bumped into some more blacks and was surprised to discover there was a girl from my own country at G.A.C. She was called Ivy, an Ashanti. She wore a not-so huge Afro, was slim and full bosomed and had a nice African rear end. She knew a Ghanaian right away when she saw one; so without my having spoken, she asked me in perfect Twi (the Ashanti language):

"Are you from Ghana?"

"Yes, but how could you tell?" I also said in Twi.

"I know every Ghanaian by appearance alone."

"You've really done nicely to recognize your countryman. I had mistaken you for a black American because of your Afro."

She smiled and I saw that she was flattered because back home, everybody, or all the students at least, liked the looks of black American girls. We had called them Afro Americans at home. Forgive me if I keep interchanging names for the African Americans. They have undergone an identify crisis of name because here are people who have been called Niggers, Negroes, colored people, Afro Americans, black people, and finally, and belatedly, African-Americans. Six names for the same people and whites have remained whites forever. I am even tempted to call him the Diasporan

African. After all, he seems not to have an identity, thanks to the white man and many centuries of painful slavery.

Ivy was happy. She was speaking Twi, her own language, seven thousand miles away from where it is spoken. I would deliberately, throw in some Fanti phrases to tell her that I was actually a Fanti, but born and bred among the Ashantis.

"How long have you been at G.A.C.?" I asked.

"I came last year as a junior."

"Why, did you transfer from another college?"

"No."

"So you are now a senior."

"Yes, are you surprised?"

"Of course, Ivy."

"I came here with three strong 'A' level grades from Wesley Girls High School, (the school of the famed Ama Ata Aidoo), so I got credit hours for two years, and I now have only a year to graduate."

"Lucky you. I also have an 'A' level certificate; but when I asked if I could have some credit hours, Dave, our registrar, said, 'No.'

"Maybe your grades weren't as good as mine otherwise, he would have given you the credit hours."

"I guess so."

I knew why my 'A' level grades were not good. Actually, they did not correspond to my brilliant academic aptitude but, dear reader, you will know why later.

"What courses are you taking?" Ivy asked.

Every college student wants to know what the other student is taking. When I told her what courses I was taking, she just gasped and shouted in a piercing sing-song soprano.

"Wow," she said in English, and asked in Twi, "Can you handle them?"

"Yes, I am a pre-medical student and I must take these courses, sooner or later."

"Oh, as a freshman, you should take some sluff courses just to settle in."

Why was everybody saying I had quite a heavy load? I was beginning to get scared. Ivy got closer to me and whispered something in my ear. In close quarters, Ivy had a slight squint in her left eye. It made her look dreamy and I liked it. Ivy wasn't any older than myself, I could tell, and I was happy that my social life wouldn't be a frustration to begin with, because here was my own beautiful girl from my country. We had much in common and we could always find an item of conversation to talk about.

"Where is your dormitory, Ivy?"

"I am in Wahlstrom 306." She turned around and pointed at the huge, cream-coloured brick dormitory.

"I will be sure to pay you a visit," I said, and we departed. When I got to class, I was late, but that didn't bother me much. I was just exulting in the fact that the world was such a small place that even at the farthest corner of the world, one is bound to meet a Ghanaian. I heard there were even Ghanaians in Greenland living in igloos.

After two class periods, the chapel bell was tolling, inviting students and the staff to service. I saw Mark outside Nobel, and we walked to Christ Chapel. Many students had settled in the pews already. The chapel was full and I was surprised at the deep religiosity of these American youths. A short service with a carefully chosen sermon was delivered by Pastor Elvee, a stocky man with a limp, not because he had one bad leg, but because the clog that he wore on his left foot was a bit worn out. We all sang some familar songs. Lutheranism is not so different from Catholicism. The service ended, and we streamed out only to resume classes once more. Mark went to his English class, and I went to my French class.

I broke class right about midday. I got a Coca-Cola from a vending machine and headed back to Co-ed. Mark was there already.

"I am going to the soccer field. Are you coming with me?"

"Yes, I will," I said and offered him the rest of my coke. He took a sip and handed it back. Actually, on my schedule, I had laboratory work in all my three classes, but somehow I had forgotten about them. I changed and went with Mark to the field. They were practicing dribbling with the coach. They played like women. I found that even with no natural skills in the game, I played like a one-eyed man among the blind. It thrilled me a lot.

Later, as the days and weeks trudged by, I went to class, neglected my laboratory afternoon schedule, went to the soccer field, ate, and slept. I was not even studying, very uncharacteristic of me because I was a bookworm.

I kept losing my keys. After three occasions of such losses, the professor who oversaw the hall got angry because I was showing my face too often to him and his wife. I was a bother to them. He got me a string, tied a key to it, put it around my neck, and told me not to be careless and lose it again because he was tired of seeing my face. I was confused. What I found myself doing most of the time was writing long letters and poems. I had never written poems before. One of the poems, which I handed to the college newspaper editor was good enough to be published. I was quite loquacious and assertive wherever I went, and kept waking up way too early. Why were all these things happening to me? Every day brought something new to my quickened personality. I was drawing more and more attention to myself. Mark took it as routine, but Eric noticed something.

"Why are you always running and whistling, brother? You must be some wild African, man."

"I must run because I am in sports," I said.

"Slow down, man. Are you alright?"

"Sure Eric, I am fine. Why do you ask?"

At that time, I never understood why Eric was watching me so closely. It didn't register anything. I was always too preoccupied to give it a thought. As I look back now, I was riding headlong into hyperactivity. Many times, I showed a quality of self-assurance, satisfaction, and extreme confidence. I was both talkative and foolishly kind with money. Later on, I seemed to be bored with routine and lacked any sustained interest in any activity. I never submitted myself to any self-examination, for I was too busy. Sometimes, I exhibited unrestrained playfulness and happiness. My speech was crisp and I was articulate in five languages. My elation stimulated ideas of grandeur, for I believed, wholeheartedly, that I would be a Nobel prize winner and would rub shoulders with the laureates who were to attend the impending conference. These were all delusions.

At my biology class one day, I told my professor that he was wrong. An argument ensued and I proved a point to him. Later in the morning, I boldly gave a tearful speech at Christ Chapel at morning service. After the service, Pastor Elvee led me straight to the school psychologist, a tall, lanky bearded and grave man. I sat in his office and he talked with me for a long time, asking occasional questions and, for the most part, listening to me talk. He told me I was sick.

"How can I be sick?"

"You are, but you don't know it."

There was a weighted throb in my heart. The casual iambic beat of my pulse became spondaic.

The school psychologist picked up the telephone on his right and dialed a quick number. He was calling the police.

"Why are you calling the police?" I asked in complete amazement and confusion.

"It is a matter of procedure."

"Have I done something wrong?"

"No, but you are sick."

"If you insist that I am sick, then call the doctor."

I was now becoming more and more afraid. A good fifteen minutes of charged silence ensued and I was in a serious state of paranoia as I heard knocking on the door. Two white police-officers, tall and fat, one with a belly pushing tightly at his belt, stepped in. Both policemen carried guns. As far as I knew, I was as harmless as a day old puppy, and I had not committed a crime, so why policemen and, for that matter, why guns?

"Just follow what they say. I am going with you to the hospital."

My fear subsided a little because the psychologist mentioned hospital. As we stepped outside with both policemen, one on each side of me, we got into the police car and sped towards a private hospital in a nearby town which I later got to know to be Mankato. It was about ten miles away.

Luckily, the psychiatrist was around and after some interviewing, he gave me a dose of a tranquilizer. It was Thorazine, and I was led to my comfortable bed in the ward. There was a color television in my room. There was a bell to call a nurse. The room was carpeted and a photo of Jesus was on the wall in front of me. On one table was a black Bible. In no time, I began to feel drowsy and fell deep in slumber, assisted by the tranquilizer. After what seemed like many hours of sleep, I was awakened by a bell to go for supper in the hospital cafeteria. The food was sumptuous. Strangely, I had a very good appetite.

There were ten of us in the cafeteria. There were two young girls, possibly sixteen years old. One was well dressed and heavily made up. The other was not too shabby, however, not as smartly dressed as the other. One young guy was in delirium, talking to himself and laughing on occasion. A middle-aged woman was pensive, and another man had brought ten novels to the cafeteria. He interchanged eating with reading, and to my surprise he was trying to read the ten books at the same time. The rest were, listlessly, picking at their food. I noticed that two of them were rocking back and forth in their chairs while also eating. I remember I ate hurriedly and went for seconds. I was hungry.

I never talked to anyone and once again, I was the only black in the group. I retired to my room and just stared at the ceiling. I was still in delusions and hallucinations. When the nurse, finally, came to my room with medication, I stood up with a start.

"Why don't you turn the TV on?"

"Sorry, I forgot it was there," I heard myself saying.

She turned it on for me and gave me two tablets and a glass of orange juice. She was a nice young nurse who always spoke sympathetically.

"How long are they going to keep me here?" I asked, because I was still worried about school.

"It will be up to the doctor to say. I think you'll go to court tomorrow and you'll formally be committed."

"Why court? What have I done?"

"You haven't done anything. You see, they can't keep you here unless it is proven in court that you are actually indisposed," she said and offered a smile displaying perfect white teeth. My anxiety dwindled.

"There is a courtroom right here in the hospital. If you get committed, don't worry. I will take care of you. I actually think you need some quiet rest here. You'll be okay. What is your name?"

"Kwame."

"That's a nice name."

I heard myself saying, "Thank you."

True to her words, the following day, the college psychologist came over with some of my clothes. I changed into new clothes and he accompanied me to court. The psychiatrist was there and he and the psychologist somehow were able to get me committed. I stayed in the hospital for two weeks while I attended both group and occupational therapy. After those weeks, I was discharged. I felt a bit better for the delusions had subsided, however not completely.

I thought I was going to be taken back to Gustavus but the college psychologist said two weeks was a long time to miss classes.

"Aren't you taking me to campus then?"

"Not now." He was always a man of a few words.

"Where will you take me then?"

He didn't answer me.

It so happened that my American father had been talked to on the telephone, so as I got out of the hospital in Mankato, he had come all the way from Alexandria to get me. The psychologist did not tell me anything, so I concluded that that was the end of my college life in the United States, short as it had been.

"Will they send me home, Dad?" I was quick to ask. The thought made me quite anxious which was bad for my recent state. Dad was quiet and that even heightened my anxiety. I knew he was very sad because somehow I had failed him by cracking up. He had very good intentions for me, for, after all, it was his money that paid for my plane trip to the United States for the second time. His hopes were rather high that I could have been a good doctor. Was he giving up already?

Chapter III

Days in St. Peter State Hospital (An Asylum)

Minnesota, most Americans will agree with me, is a very cold place during winter. In fact, the coldest town in the continental United States, International Falls, which constantly registers below zero degree weather in winter, is found in this state. Indian summer was soon to give way to brisk breezes with a chill in them and the way of dressing had changed in response to this. Everybody knew that the warmth of summer and fall had ended and that the inevitable monstrous cold winter of Minnesota was lurking not far off.

After a week with my American father at Alexandria, where he tried very hard to fill me with renewed confidence for school and courage to brace the new life's struggle ahead of me due to the transition of the previous chapter; he picked a basketball and tried a few shots himself, old as he was.

"Kwame, come on, pick the ball and give it a shot."

"Thank you, but I can't play basketball. I'd rather sit in the living room and watch TV, and I am not feeling very well as you know."

"Take your mind off that! You can't gain anything by taking solace in sickness and using it as an excuse. Face the world."

That terse sentence, "Face the world," stuck in my troubled mind there and then, and it has been my attitude towards life since then. I came out and took some shots and, surprisingly, I made a few baskets. Dad was good at almost everything with wiry hands he made some deft shots, and while at it he said, "Kwame, you are going to St. Peter tomorrow."

I brightened up from my sullenness and asked, "Am I going back to school?"

"Not right away, son."

Dad collected the ball from me and placed his hand on my shoulder as he decided to let us walk to the mailbox. He had just seen the mailman.

"You are going to sit out this semester and start everything over again during January."

"Does that mean that I am just going to lazy around at G.A.C. doing nothing for the rest of the semester?" I asked, quite anxious.

"No, son ... "

"Then, where will I stay?" I cut in to wring the answer from him because I was excited that at least there was still a chance of my attending college.

"It so happens that there is a hospital at St. Peter. As a matter of fact, it is a state hospital where people with your kind of problem are helped to recuperate and recover completely."

"I don't undertand. How can I be in a hospital bed again when I am not sick?"

"I know you don't Kwame. It isn't a hospital as you know of. There is everything there. It is almost a rooming house with grounds, a library, a church, and a cafeteria. You will love it when you go there."

"I will be very lonely ... "

"Oh, St. Peter State Hospital is just about a mile and a half away from Gustavus. The school psycologist will get your friends to visit you on and off."

"How did you get all the information, Dad?"

"Don't worry, son, I have been talking to the psychologist."

My fears soon gave way to hope. I was looking forward to seeing this hospital talked about by dad and even more anxious to live there for the next couple of months.

The next day, my American mom, who had returned from Wisconsin the previous day, got up very early, cooked breakfast, gave me some comforting words, and off we were in Dad's Brougham. I slept most of the way because I was still on the tranquilizers.

As we neared St. Peter, dad stopped at a hamburger joint and bought me a juicy deluxe hamburger and a milkshake. Soon, we were in the confines of St. Peter State Hospital. I was immediately struck by the immense old redbrick buildings and the solitude of the environment. Soon, we were climbing a gentle slope after we passed the green and white sign of St. Peter State Hospital. Up the hill and to the right, was a huge, red administration building. Dad stopped the car and went in to inquire something. After some ten minutes, he was back and drove to another huge, red brick building

"This is where you are going to stay, Kwame," Dad said. "It is your ward."

We went inside and after a few bureaucracies, a nurse ushered me to my room. The place was quiet, which gave me an eerie feeling. Dad comforted me and gave me some money and a warm smile.

"Take it easy in here Kwame."

"I will, Dad, don't worry."

"No, I am worried about you worrying."

"Okay, I won't."

When Dad left, I almost cried, but I remembered I was a young man so many thousands of miles from my indigenous home. Therefore, I should try very hard not to compound my problem by feeling too lonely too soon. I took my coat off and went out of the room to survey my new environment.

Immediately, I was accosted by a not-too-young lady by the name of Donna.

"Hi," she said.

"Hi," I said back and a bit afraid, which I shouldn't have been.

"Where are you from?"

"Gustavus."

"No, your country 'cus you speak with an accent."

"How can you tell I have an accent, because I have only said two words to you."

"I was right; you really have an accent. You must be from Africa," she said and gave a silly laugh.

"Yes, why?"

"Nothing."

"C'mon, you were so interested to talk to me. Now you say, 'nothing.'"

"Oh, nothing," she said again and puffed on her cigarette which, obviously, she didn't know how to smoke well, and continued to stare at me blankly.

After some coaxing, she came to from her severe stare and said, "I studied the geography of West Africa in school ... "

With the mention of West Africa, I cut in and said, "Oh, I come from Ghana."

I was surprised to hear Donna talking about cocoa, gold, and even Kwame Nkrumah. After some time, she asked "Why are you here, you must have cracked up?" She smiled. She was the first person to use the phrase "cracked up" and at that time I didn't understand it, so I asked calmly,

"What is 'cracked up'?"

"You've gone bananas.'"

"I still don't understand."

"Then you were 'nuts.'"

"Donna, we are speaking English, but I don't understand your language."

"Oh, you were 'loonie.'"

"Donna!"

"You went 'cuckoo.'"

"Are you pulling my leg or what?" I was getting angry and I could see Donna was not deterred by her strange confrontation. When she saw that I was getting flustered, she felt sorry because she thought she was only playing games with me.

"I am sorry, Kwame. You were mentally sick, and if you don't understand that too, you were crazy."

When I heard the last phrase, a heavy throb almost succeeded in giving me a cardiac arrest.

"Me, mentally sick ... no! Not crazy, not me!"

"Yes, this is where all of them are."

Donna "hit the nail on the head" for me because all along I did not exactly know or I hadn't accepted that I was sick in spite of the fact that I had been in a hospital in Mankato, seen the psychologist and the psychiatrist, and was out of school. A deep sense of ignominious shame befell me.

"Why me?" I asked.

Donna put it better and said, "Why us?"

Tears instantly blurred my eyes. If there was any sickness I feared the most in life, it was mental illness. No illness is good for humanity, but this one was looked upon with such debasement that I considered my young life wrecked. How was I to use this same "crazy" mind, my only gift in life (the gift God gave me was academic intelligence)? How was I to study with this same stressed mind to become a doctor? I had a big problem which I thought would annihiliate my future, but I remembered Dad's words of "Face the world," and I knew I was in for a life's struggle. Ideas of death and suicide crossed my mind.

"Won't I be better dead than with a monstrous problem like this hovering over my life?"

I left Donna dumbstruck because of my sudden change from cheerful confidence to sullenness. I went to my room, buried my head in my pillow, and cried tons of tears. In my preoccupation with crying and feeling sorry for myself, I missed supper.

Donna, a real glutton, (you could tell from her hefty figure with three spare tires on each side of the stomach and a bulging belly), had brought some slices of bread and cold cuts and a huge banana which she said was for the night. Kindness overcame her and she offered me the food. With her own quarter, she bought me a can of pop, and sat and stared as I ate. She finally broke her stare and said either sadly or happily-- I could not tell, "Kwame, I am institutionalized."

"What?"

"It means, I get to spend all my life here in the hospital."

At that time, in America, mentally sick people were just put away in institutions (state hospitals) never to come back and mingle with the so-called sane society. Malcolm X's mother suffered this horrible fate.

"Why, Donna?"

"Well, they say I can't get back to society."

"Who says so?"

"The doctor and the nurses."

"How long have you been here, Donna?"

"Ten years."

At the mention of ten years, my heart sank a heavy throb and missed a couple of beats. Was I going to be institutionalized too and be here for this length of time? I remembered my dad's words that I was going to stay out only one semester and go back to college, but was he a doctor or a nurse to say this?

Donna knew I was worried about something, but she couldn't put my mind to rest, and after I finished eating my supper that she had kindly brought me, she left.

Later, when I had been in the hospital for some days, Donna left me alone and wouldn't even say hi to me. I thought I had offended her, but the nurses confided in me that it was her habit of seemingly making good friends with new admissions, but later withdrew to herself and kept feeling depressed afterwards.

The next day was a Tuesday when I was supposed to meet the doctor. In the morning, the nurses gave me an electric razor, aftershave cologne, and spray deodorant for my morning shower and toilet. At that time, I didn't understand why I was given the electric razor, for I had no hairs on my face. Maybe it was for my armpits, but I knew that the Americans, especially, the men, didn't shave their armpits. I used it anyway for my underarms because in Ghana it was outrageous for both men and women to have hairs in the armpits, and the pubic area. We considered that unclean. I splashed the cologne lavishly on myself although I never had any body odors, and I was really smelling nice indeed.

The doctor was ready for me in his office at nine. He was a short, stocky man with well-greased hair and abundant black beard. Even in my recent state, I could see he was a nervous man because he couldn't do without chain smoking. His eyes were dark, piercing, and probing which gave an indication that he wanted to know everything about me. After he used his last finger to cause the ash on his cigarette to fall into the ashtray, he smiled encouragingly and offered me a seat on a couch in his somehow comfortable office.

"Thank you, sir," I said.

"Your name is Kwame, I gather."

"Yes, sir."

"According to your file, you've been quite sick lately."

"Yes, I never really knew I was sick, although I was going through a lot. A patient in this hospital, Donna, put it in real layman's terms, that I was mentally sick or literally crazy."

"Do you admit it now?"

"I guess I should because here I am in a mental hospital."

"That's very good. Your sickness was diagnosed as manic-depression by your former doctor and I agree with him."

"Sir, please, what is manic-depression and what causes it?"

"Manic-depression is a type of psychosis that is characterized by wide mood swings. By the way, does anybody in your family, past or present, have a mental problem?"

"Not that I know of now, but why, sir?"

"The reason why is that heredity has a predisposing factor in the causation of manic-depression," the doctor said and sent a huge coil of smoke to dangle between us. He crumpled the unfinished butt in the ashtray. I coughed, and he apologized and didn't smoke for the rest of the interview, much to his discomfort.

"Doctor, will this bout, happen again?" I asked with a lot of butterflies in my stomach.

"It may or not be chronic, but whatever the case, I am going to put you on medication."

"For how long will that continue because, Doctor, I never take drugs of any kind, prescribed or not."

"You might have to take it for the rest of your life."

My heart missed a couple of beats again when I heard the doctor.

"Why, Doctor?"

"Your new situation warrants it and you must get used to it."

My eyes were blurred with unshed tears. Noticing this, the doctor offered me a couple of paper tisues to dab my eyes.

"No need for crying. Would you like to be sick all the time or would you like a different course in life? The medication will help you. In fact, I have prescribed Lithium Carbonate and Haloperidol for your daily use."

This time I was sobbing uncontrollably. The doctor let me cry to vent the depressed emotion.

After a while, he said, "C'mon, Kwame, taking medication is not the end of your life. It is only a novel situation which you will by all means get used to, but remember to take the medication always."

I sat confused for some long seconds and said, "I will take them, Doctor."

"That's a good boy. Wipe your face and cheer up. Make that a promise for me."

"It's a promise, Doctor."

"If so, then you'll be out of here soon."

"That means I am not going to be institutionalized like Donna."

"Oh, no, Kwame, rest assured you are not."

"Thanks."

After this, the doctor did a routine physical check-up and told me I was physically very healthy. I was encouraged.

"If you have any problems, don't hesitate to talk to the nurse. Alright?"

"Yes, Doctor."

"You may go."

"Thank you, sir."

I put on my clothes, put my glasses on, the doctor held the door open for me, and I left his office. As I stepped out, I could hear the clicking sound of a lighter. The doctor had lighted himself a much awaited cigarette. In my mind's eye, I knew I was sick, but others were sick too- for why should people smoke and, for that matter, why should a doctor? In any case, after some time in the hospital, I saw that the patients were given cigarettes after meals. It's surprising that today I don't smoke, for I really had a good opportunity to smoke in St. Peter State Hospital. Whenever I was offered cigarettes, I would take them and give them to blondish Patty, a seventeen year old, perhaps drug addict, who had no qualms pestering me to be her boyfriend. Patty had a beautiful sweet face. Her smile released a pair of deep dimples that always enhanced her beauty. From the way she dressed and made up, you could tell she came from a rich family.

I always wondered why Patty had cracked up so early in life. She had been in the hospital a year already. She had razor cuts on her left arm. She told me several times that she wanted to die, so that explains why she pretended to commit suicide with all those small cuts.

Her level of eroticism was high and a lot of her hormonal estrogen was flowing and built up perhaps bringing her sexual hunger to a hilt. She saw me as the macho man to satisfy her sexual fancies. She was the first to introduce me to the tunnels of St. Peter State Hospital.

"Come, Kwame, I will show you something," she said and offered a real seductive smile with an eye insinuation.

"Have you seen the tunnels here?"

"No, where are they?"

"Come on, I will show you."

Patty had an ulterior motive. Love or lust was universal and Patty was crazy about me, so she led me hand in hand to the tunnel. It was a lonely passageway which connected different parts of the hospital and was mainly busy during the winter snowy months. It was well heated.

"Do you have things like this in Africa?"

"Not really."

"Well, you are seeing one today. Aren't you glad that your guide is a real winner?"

"Patty, behave."

She was quiet for a while as she snuggled beside me. She took me to a dark corner and said, "You can ball me here."

"What!"

Her bluntness surprised me, but she had led to this all along.

"Patty, we are young. What if you become pregnant?"

"Kwame, you are so ignorant. Don't you know the girls here are given birth control pills just in case?"

"Really, I am surprised, so they encourage sex too, let alone smoking. Patty, I am afraid I have never done it before."

"Me neither, but I want to do it today. I surrender my whole body to you. You can touch me. I've waited for this for too long and you came along. I love you."

"As for today, a beautiful white girl loves a poor African boy who is supposedly crazy, something indeed."

"Some of your people hated us for a long time and some still do. I am actually scared to love you."

"Kwame, I am ashamed to call those bastards (past or present) my people. I said I love you, and I really mean it, okay!"

"Don't yell at me, Patty. Cool down. If my first time is going to be with a white virgin, I really don't mind. I never dreamt of it."

Patty smiled and said, "It's about time you stopped arguing." She unbuttoned her blouse without any coyness and there, hiding under the blouse, were those white succulent and protuberant pearshapes with pink tits. She finally aroused me, and I possessed her with a lot of initial fumbling of a sexual rookie. Patty was satisfied that I did it with her, and she later guarded our love jealously to the dismay and astonishment of the nurses who did everything to keep us from each other.

After doing it with Patty, the devilish, almighty, guilty feeling overcame me; however, there was a Catholic priest on Sunday to whom I confessed my sins. I wanted to be freed from the heavy weight of my conscience just because I had compromised my religion and impeccable morals and sinned. I think God will forgive two mentally ill people who, due to their illness, had done wrong. As I look back, there seemed to be sexual indiscretions with both male and female patients. Guilt overcame them when they got better.

A week and a half after my admission, there was also a new admission, a middle-aged man named Joe who, at first glance, looked like a simpleton. He wasn't. He was restless and talkative. Immediately he saw me, he gave me a twenty-dollar bill. Joe was not satisfied with the twenty dollars so he called me again and gave me another twenty dollars because he said I was a poor African. Surprising how the mentally sick can be so carelessly genial with money.

"Not every African is poor," I said.

"But you are, so have it."

I took the money and thanked him.

"Never mind," he said.

When he went to play the piano in the ward, he would play several pieces non-stop; and to my untrained ears, I could tell he was a virtuoso. He did a great deal of improvisation too, and that was why I said he wasn't a simpleton. At times, when Joe talked to me, he would be trembling, unshed tears came into his eyes, and, sometimes, he would cry loudly with real tears on his cheeks. A moment later, however, he would be laughing as if very happy. I never understood crying and laughing so close to each other, but I was told it was characteristic of bipolar, manic-depression. These are definitely mood swings.

It was nearing mid-December. As Minnesota has the most capricious climate in America, snow had already fallen and melted. I had gone out to dabble in the flaccid snow, and my shoes felt wet. It was my second season of seeing snow and that confirmed the fact that I was really in a temperate region of the world.

Had it not been for Patty, hospital life would have been a real bore; we did nothing much. Our day usually started with medication, which we always took with orange juice. We went to breakfast around 7:30 A.M. There were always small boxes of cornflakes and sugar crispies and bowls of hot cereal. We took theses with milk, any number of slices of toast and superfluous butter, a choice of orange juice, prune juice, apple juice or tomato juice, and fried or scrambled eggs. My best days were when we had pancakes and syrup and bacon for breakfast. The pancakes were large circles, usually steaming hot. Butter melted quickly and seeped into their pores. I would go for seconds, thirds and fourths. Patty, who always ate with me, was surprised and wondered where I stashed all the pancakes. Patty would eat only a quarter pancake, a slice of bacon, and a glass of milk. She said she was watching her weight. I never gained weight no matter how much I ate, and felt sorry for Patty and most American women who have so much to eat but preferred not to just because they would gain weight. It sounded so paradoxical to me.

After breakfast, we sometimes went for occupational therapy until about 11:45 A.M. when the bell would ring again for lunch. Our lunch sometimes consisted of noodle hot dishes, sometimes beef stroganoff, macaroni and cheese, all of which I hated with a passion. When it was time for chicken, then I was a happy man because I would gobble down quite carelessly huge chunks of both white and dark meat. On chicken and pancakes days, I would eat so much that I had to miss the next meal by all means.

Sunday's supper was usually cold cuts and I would eat delectably because, to me, it was quite gratifying to have only protein for a meal. All in all, the food, except for the noodle hot dishes, was not all that bad.

Since I was given pocket money at the hospital, I usually walked with Patty to go and buy ice cream at the store which served the mobile homes along the main highway, after every evening meal. I knew ice cream was fattening, but hunger-ravaged Patty in the midst of plenty would eat it anyway.

It was nearing Christmas and the hospital had been decorated with pine trees and flashing lights at every corner. It was this time that the school psychologist got the few friends I had made at college to visit me. Ivy had prepared a sumptuous peanut butter soup with chicken. She was looking good with her Afro well combed. She had a small mirror in which she, occasionally, looked at herself. Eric was there and, yes, he was talking, gesticulating and smiling. Mark brought me some candy.

"I am still waiting for you to come back, Kwame," Mark said and smiled.

"Thanks, but I don't come till next semester."

"How about January term?" Mark asked and took a piece of chicken from my soup. Ivy offered him a paper napkin.

"I've been told I would stay here and walk to school."

"Are you kidding?" You can do three miles every day in this cold, snow, and ice?"

"Well, I have no other choice."

"I suppose you said you've lived one winter in Minnesota, so you know what to expect."

It was getting late. The psychologist had left already and Eric drove Mark and Ivy back in his blue Chevrolet after they had said good-bye.

I was quite refreshed by that visit and, surely, I couldn't wait to get back to school.

Chapter IV

Second Christmas in America

On December 21, Mr. Aga, my American father, came to the hospital for me to spend Christmas with the whole Aga family at Alexandria. I was very pleased to see him and we got back to Alexandria in good time in spite of the snow.

The house was well-decorated for Christmas. The ubiquitous pine Christmas trees were flashing with red, yellow, blue and white lights. Snow was already on the ground and we were all set for a white Christmas, the dream of every Minnesotan. The kitchen was exuding wonderful aromas from Mom's cooking. She was a real gourmet. She had cooked up some pork chops and baked potatoes with sauce and gravy. I helped to set the table with Rob, my American brother. After Rob lit the couple of candles on the table, I poured cold water into the crystal glasses. A Handel oratorio was playing on Dad's stereo and the serene aura was perfect. We sat down for dinner where Dad was subtle with well-chosen good humor to cheer his African son up. I smiled gleefully and that fortified me with good mental health. Surely, Dad and his family had a way of cheering me up. After dinner, Dad asked, "Kwame, how would you like to go for a short walk around Lake Darling?"

"Sure, Dad, I wouldn't mind that at all."

Actually, I was stuffed and could do with a walk. Dad put his London Fog coat and a hat on. Rob gave me one of his woolen coats, a Viking stocking cap, and some woolen gloves. He joined us and we were on the highway along Lake Darling. It was cold, but we were comfortably dressed.

28

The snow on the ground was soft. We left footprints behind us as we walked along. Dad broke the silence and asked, "Kwame, are you enjoying your second Christmas in America? I am enjoying it. Aren't you, Rob?"

"I am enjoying it right now with you, but I wish I weren't sick," I said.

"Oh, Kwame, you'll be okay," Rob said.

"Yes, people have undergone what you are going through and come out alright. Just have faith and take your medication," Dad said.

"I am thinking about college and … "

"Kwame, take one thing at a time. Get fully recovered first. We shall all do our best to help you," Dad said.

"Thank you."

"Just take it easy, Kwame," Rob said.

"Look! There is a car going over Lake Darling. Is it well-frozen over?" I asked.

"I think so, Kwame. Don't you see the fish houses already?" Rob said.

"I guess I do, but I was afraid for the driver. I thought the ice wasn't thick enough."

"That should give you an idea of how cold it is and is going to be for the winter. Are you worried about January term walking back and forth to the hospital?"

"Yes, I am."

"Kwame, you are tough. Don't worry. Do you remember how we met?" Dad asked.

"Yes, I was running in the snow and cold, training for track at that time."

"We were all surprised that you, an African from the tropics, could go outside and run. We were all inside enjoying our heated rooms. That makes you tough, Kwame," Rob said.

"Thank you very much. Now I don't fear anymore to do the three miles."

"That's the way to go," Dad said.

We crossed the bridge spanning the creek and the highway and walked about the lake facing the road which went towards Arrowwood Lodge. We turned around and walked across the railway tracks and headed towards Lake Cowdry, intending to say hi to the Godfreys, who were family friends. The Godfreys were at home watching television. Immediately they saw us, Mrs. Godfrey offered us some coffee and cookies. I had wanted to decline the offer but for courtesy's sake, I took the refreshment and ate a couple of cookies and drank the black sugarless coffee. That made me even more stuffed.

"How would you like a game of ping pong?" Mr. Godfrey challenged me, as he was always used to doing whenever I chanced to come to his house. I thought I could use the exercise so I said, "You had better get your smashing paddles ready or else … "

"Oh, you think you can beat me again, eh?"

"You better believe it, Pa Godfrey."

The table was already fitted with the net and two newly bought cushion paddles were ready for us. Dad and Rob decided to come to the basement and watch us play. We started a very gentlemanly game with Pa Godfrey having a slight edge to win the first game. With a lot of initial fumbling, I succeeded in pulling one game back and we were all satisfied with the score. We, therefore, stopped for another day.

I was relieved from the gluttony of late after the game and also hot. I came out briefly into the cold, and in no time I was shivering violently. I went to join Dad, Rob, and the Godfreys as we talked about Africa and the cold weather. I was already forgetting my sickness, and I was really cheered. These Alexandrians of Minnesota really had a very good disposition of bringing comfort to this young African. After being at the Godfreys a while longer, Dad asked leave of them and we headed back home. It was already dark. It had been a very good day. In bed that night I prayed a lengthy prayer for God to give me more days like this one.

On the 22nd of December, my American sister, Marilyn, arrived with her husband and her two sons, Michael and Robb. Marilyn brought along some presents and the Christmas tree was glittering with well-wrapped boxes of shiny wrapping paper. I was wondering what presesnts these very kind people would give me.

Christmas day was awaited with real anxiety. In spite of the snow and the cold weather, people were really frantic with their shopping. The big shops were full to the brim with shoppers. Downtown Alexandria was a sight to see, for there had been decorations all along the main streets. At night, the different colored lights flickered as if they were on one big Christmas tree. The temperature was about ten degrees below zero. All was set for a really cold, white Christmas, the great desire of most Minnesotans.

Christmas Eve came with a bang. Dad had, somehow, got the outfit for Santa Claus. The little ones were itching to see him. Of course, they hadn't the slightest idea who Santa Claus would be. Christmas carols were blasting everywhere. At about nine o'clock in the night, Santa Claus arrived with his deep "Ho ho!" and a bag full of presents. Michael, Scott, and Robb were picked onto Santa Claus' lap and given some wonderful current toys. After that, Mom took a wrapped present, one after the other, and gave them to Santa Claus to present to those who had been good all year. Luckily, I was one of them.

I got many presents of warm woolen socks, gloves, a stocking cap, a camera, a photo album and a nice pair of trousers and a shirt. I wasn't expecting this demonstration of love at all, and I saw that really I was getting better, almost my old self with my whimsical sense of humor. I couldn't help cracking a joke or two.

I slept late that evening with convivial conversations with everybody. Everybody was particular in making Kwame "one of us" and I was grateful.

We were all up in time to attend church service at Mom and Dad's Lutheran church. After church service, we went straight to Arrowwood Lodge for Dad's treat. I just couldn't believe the appetizing and delicious cuisine that lay in wait for us. We all sat on a very big round table with a carefully chosen white tablecloth, crystal glasses, china for coffee, and candles. The aura was serene. I could not believe my eyes when the huge, roasted juicy lamb was brought to the table by smartly dressed waiters and waitresses. They filled our glasses with wine and carved the mutton. It was all so serene that I couldn't believe it was Kwame, the poor, recently deranged African who was receiving such sophisticated warmth and attention. I later discovered that Dad had planned all this because of me.

After Christmas, I rested for some three days and Dad and I went back to St. Peter State Hospital. The hospital was having its own warm Christmas festivity for the patients and even Joe was in good spirits. I was a happy man but some more of the good cheer still trickled down to me.

As I was enjoying myself, I was also thinking about the January term which was going to start on the 4th of January. Immediately we celebrated the New Year; the fourth of January came as if there was no day between the New Year and the fourth. The laborious task had begun.

I wore my thermal underwear and put on my great woolen coat. I had assumed a size twice my own. I had signed up for Horticulture, so I got my textbook and an exercise book and set upon my one and a half miles of cold, snow and ice. I took the longer way of the main highway. That day the snow and ice had not been plowed, so at some places I fell knee deep into the snow. I never met anybody on the way. All around, the place was marvelously white with a few yellow patches here and there. I knew there had been some stray dogs around.

Slowly, I went away from the highway and I was climbing the steep hill to the entrance of Gustavus Adolphus. I reached my classroom at exactly ten past eight. The professor had already filled the blackboard with notes and was explaining away. I took off my coat and scarf and sat to fill my exercise book with the notes, at the same time listening to the explanation of the professor. Luckily, my friends, Mark and Phil, were in the same class. They came to me when the class was over. I took a trip with them to my room on third floor Co-ed. Mark had kept all my things intact. My photographs and track medals were all there.

We talked at length over happenings during the past semester. Mark brought a present from his mom and dad, and Phil assured me that they were all willing to help to make school life better.

Since none of them had a car, I had to trudge back to St. Peter State Hospital on foot. It was a lonely journey, but I took consolation from the fact that I was going to meet more warmth from Patty, Joe, and others.

"How was your day?" Patty asked while she took my books and helped me out of my coat.

"Cold and slippery," I said.

"Oh, you can handle it, Kwam."

"True, I did make it today, hurrah!"

"Oh, Kwame, it won't be that bad. I am always here to help," Patty said.

"Patty, you are getting better from the way you speak. If you keep it up, you are going to be out of here pretty quick."

"Thanks, Kwam, but I hope to leave here the same time you do."

"I hope to get out of this bin by the end of January. Our term would have ended by then. Can you wait that long?"

"Kwam, I have had a test of patience for over two years. I can wait it out through these last weeks. The doctor said I was doing better. I hope you'll help me to get out of here."

"My help will compliment yours. Hopefully, we'll all be out of here soon. You know we don't belong here, and we have our whole youthful lives ahead of us."

Things went pretty well for me for a week or two. However, I will never forget the nineteenth of January when I was caught in a blizzard. I had walked in the cold overcast skies until I reached the mobile homes a little way up the highway. It started to snow gradually and later thickly, which made visibility impossible. The cold, biting wind picked up its blowing intensity. I felt like seeking shelter somewhere, at least in one of the mobile homes where I could see fluorescent lights shining through the apparent lack of visibility, caused by the heavily falling snow. The snow on the ground was thickening by the second and by every flake of snow. I was in a quandary whether to turn around to the hospital, or continue to school. It was then that I realized that I had made a blunder that day by not wearing the right type of boots. My feet were numb and I was afraid that I might get frost-bitten.

I tried as much as possible to move forward because I had less than a mile to go. Walking in the deep snow was not fun, and it was made all the more difficult by the fact that every step I took sank me further to my knees and deeper into the snow. Occasionally, I would fall flat on my face. Why had I not received any warning of the impending snow storm that day? I never ran across a car whose driver might have had sympathy on me to give me a break and a ride from that blustery winter day.

I walked slowly up the hill to the college and upon arrival at my class there was not a soul there and I had not met anyone really on the way. It soon dawned on me that classes had been canceled due to the snow storm. With much more difficulty, I walked from Nobel Auditorium towards Co-ed. The "Tundra" in front of Co-ed was a white riot with most of the cars at the park covered almost to the top with snow. Snow banks were almost up to the second floor windows. When I got the door opened, a waft of warm air greeted my arrival into the dormitory.

I climbed up to my room and, fortunately, Mark was there.

"Why, Kwame, didn't you know that there was going to be a snow storm?"

"How could I know? There aren't any radios in the hospital and I thought I shouldn't miss class."

"Classes are cancelled for today, Kwame."

"I know. I went to our class first and there was nobody there."

"I don't think you should make the return journey to the hospital."

"Well, of course, I shouldn't."

My frozen face, fingers, and toes started to thaw after I took off my coat. It was painful.

"Can I get you something hot to drink from the vending machine?"

"Yes, thanks."

"What would you like? Coffee or hot chocolate?"

"Hot chocolate with some marshmallows, Mark."

Mark left the room momentarily and came back with a cup of hot chocolate and a fat doughnut.

"Here you go , Kwame."

"Thank you."

A gentle sip sent waves of warmth down my throat all the way into my stomach. The warm room and the hot drink were slowly making me feel comfortable. It was still snowing lightly outside. I got into my bed and covered myself with my warm blankets. Mark gave me an extra one and talked to me until I fell sound asleep. Mark didn't wake me up for lunch because he said he, himself, didn't feel like walking in the deep snow.

When I woke up, we still went to the vending machine and Mark, with his own money, again bought me a few goodies which tied me up until supper.

It had stopped snowing finally, and the grounds workers were busily plowing the snow from the common walking paths and roads for the students.

"Kwame, I have ordered pizza with pepperoni and mushrooms and cheese. How's that for supper? After what you've been through today, you don't need to go out again till tomorrow."

In about twenty minutes, someone was knocking at our door with the steaming pizza. There were two big cups of cold Coca Cola.

We ate delectably and talked more.

"Kwame, we shall have our examination in Horticulture in less than ten days. How are you preparing for it?"

"You know, Mark I can't study in the hospital."

"Why don't you get one of the patients to help you study?"

"What can she do?"

"Oh, its a she, eh?"

"Yes, Patty. Didn't you meet her?"

"No, tell me more!"

"She happens to be my girlfriend in the hospital."

"Who was that, man?" Someone sounded like Eric who was obviously interrupting.

"It's me, Eric, Kwame."

"Come on in, Eric," Mark said.

"Gees, Kwam, you are looking mighty good, man."

"Thanks, Eric."

"Why are you here so late? Are you back with us already?"

"No, Eric. it's because of the snow and Mark doesn't want me to go back till tomorrow."

"Excuse me, Kwame, I've got some chick waiting for me in my room, hey, hey, hey!"

"Wow, you are lucky," Mark said.

"See you tomorrow, Kwam. I just heard your voice and couldn't wait to pop in to say hi."

"Thanks for stopping in."

I slept the night in my dormitory with my very kind roommate. I could not sleep well because I had foregone my medication. It was here I realized that the drugs really helped in bringing me my nightly sleep. Morning never seemed to come along that night, and I tossed and turned.

When finally, dawn came, I was fast asleep and Mark had to wake me to prepare for breakfast and class. When I was ready after having taken a hot shower, we walked on the ploughed paths across the "Tundra" to the school cafeteria. We went through a quick meal and headed straight to Nobel Auditorium.

As usual, I copied the notes which the professor had liberally filled on the blackboard and listened. Professor Hamrum had a whimsical sense of humor, and he interjected the lecture with several clever and humorous remarks. After the lecture, Mark accompanied me to the gate and I was a lonely bird again, with only the snow, the steep descent of the hill, and the road as my friends. Snow banks were high on both sides of the road. The road had been salted and sanded; however, it was still rather slippery on certain stretches. I managed to reach the hospital without having fallen once.

"Cheapers, Kwam, where have you been? I was worried about you." Patty was the first to greet me.

"I was caught in the snowstorm yesterday, but I survived it. Can't you see?"

"Sure, Kwam, but you must have gone through a lot. Let me help you with your coat."

"Thanks, Patty."

"Tell me more about the storm, snowman!"

"Snowman is an understatement. I was more than that."

"What makes you like school so much that you even had to go yesterday! Didn't you know anything about the storm?"

"You asked me two questions. Firstly, it's because of school that I came all the way from Africa, and I don't want to annihilate my future by being truant. And, I just didn't know a thing about the storm whatsoever."

"Poor you, we were worried stiff about you, and I missed you and your smile and humor."

"You wanna bet? Come let me show you something."

Patty walked me to my room and there were all the meals she had brought into my room while I was away.

"Gee, Patty, thanks. Now I know you really care for me."

I stretched on my bed and Patty sat on the bed too.

"How would you like to help me study?"

"How can I help? I am at your service."

"Just read my textbook and notes to me. I believe hearing them from you, I will absorb everything."

"No problem, Kwam."

"Should we start now?"

"Sure."

Patty took my notes first and began to read. She read slowly for the next thirty minutes when I stopped her. It was time for lunch. We both went and joined the already long line of patients.

With the experience of the past day, I always pestered the nurses to tell me about the weather forecasts. Fortunately, there were no more blizzards for the rest of the month.

Patty helped me with my studies every day. When we were bored, we took a trip around the tunnel, but not for sex because of the initial guilty feeling. Occasionally, we ran across some handcuffed prisoners who were in a prison close to the hospital and some retarded children who also had a ward in the hospital. Their attitude and behavior made me frightened a bit, thinking that a prolonged stay in the hospital will make me like one of them. Patty explained that they came into this world retarded, or they might have had an accident of some sort. Therefore, without accidents, intelligent people like us, though we had suffered psychosis before, will never turn retarded all of a sudden. My fears were allayed.

My first real examination in a United States college was on the twenty-ninth. The week prior to the date, Patty was really giving me a helping hand in studying. She would read to me and ask me a lot of very intelligent questions. It was then that I realized, considering my own rate of academic absorption and Patty's questions, that some psychosis do not detract or have any bearing on one's intelligence as mistakenly thought by many a layman. Even intelligent people like Van Gogh and Tchaikovsky suffered from psychosis.

I could also tell that Patty was far better; at least she never seemed to be depressed and helping me was a joy to her. She realized that she could be useful after all. This whipped up her good mental health spirits. I was doing much better. Only my being in the hospital told me that I had been sick. I knew by intuition that both of us were on our way out of the hospital, which Ken Kesey called the "Cuckoo's Nest." I just couldn't understand why this author should give a derogatory name to hospitals which endeavor to help people gain back their tarnished sanity.

The night before the test, I slept late with Patty always by my side and giving me a helping hand. She went through all my notes with me. The next morning, I found myself with a lot of academic rearmament to tackle my first test in a United States college. I arrived at the college about thirty minutes early and went immediately to my room where Mark and I went over our notes as quickly as we could.

We got to the classroom to meet anxiety written over everybody's face, for we had known and heard that Dr. Hamrum was a very tough tester. When Professor Hamrum joked that no one would pass his examination if the person had not studied hard, I prayed and took my question paper.

Thanks to Patty, the test was not tough as said by the professor. I went through the test and finished ten minutes early. I went over it, and was sure that I was going to get an A.

"How was the test?" Patty asked when I got to the hospital.

"Terrible," I joked.

"Really, how was it? You were able to do it, weren't you?"

"Yes, I was only kidding. I thought I did well."

"Thank God."

Two days later, I went to the college and got my grade from my professor, and it was an A. Surely, crazy people are also intelligent. When Patty heard of it, she was very proud of me, and of her help which was not wasted.

"I want to tell you something. You wanna hear it, Kwam?"

"I always miss your bright smile when you go to school, but that's not it. Take another guess. Can't you see I'm happy and full of smiles?'

"Oh, you get to get out of here."

"Yes Kwam, you knew it. The doctor said so."

"When?"

"As soon as my parents can come to get me."

"Have you called them?"

"Sure, Kwam. They said tomorrow or the day after. Oh, Kwam, I will miss you."

"I will also miss you. But we can always keep in touch and you could occasionally pay me a visit. What will you be doing?"

"Go back to school, of course."

"That's a good idea, but I will advise you to take it easy to avoid relapses."

"Oh, this time, I won't play with my medication and I resolve not to take any hard drugs again. That's it with me."

"Good."

"Always pray for me," Patty said.

"I will, but I also need prayer too."

While we talked the college psychologist came to the hospital and informed me that the doctor had given the okay for my discharge. He said he would come for me the next day. I felt elated. So my bout with psychosis was over. Thank God. The psychologist advised me not to be too elated because it could happen again.

Chapter V

Early Childhood in Africa

Before I go on to tell you more, I must inform the reader that I was hospitalized on five more occasions in both undergraduate and graduate schools. But let's take a look at life, which nobody knows its goal and when it will end, except of course the one who is going to commit suicide. Life is full of struggles, disappointments, and many total joys which we seem to take for granted. Let us look at the childhood which maybe was instrumental in bringing this dreaded psychosis.

My parents were Fantis from the small coastal town of Anomabo, a fishing village along the coast of Ghana. My mother is called Araba Assieduwa and my father (now long dead) was Kwame Bosomafi.

My mother always tells me that I was a proud boy from birth because I was fussy and didn't like so many things. I hated it when I was given a bath. I hated it when I wasn't breast fed in time. I hated it when I got the hiccups (which I always got), and I hated it even when I had a bowel movement. Mother said I was born at Mrs. Quartey Papafio's on one Saturday in December, 1953. She was my mother's midwife and she said she really had a battle with me the very first day I was born, when she was giving me my routine bath. I squealed and squealed and kicked. Mrs. Papafio admitted she had never delivered anyone so battle ready from the day go.

Many newborn babies look ugly to me, but mother said I was a beautiful little baby. She said my face was broad, a not-so-squashed nose, and a lot of thick curly jet black hair adorned my head, and my eyes and pupils were in a direct contrast because the pupils were jet black, surrounded by the immaculately white cornea. Mother said she loved to see my eyes but I, also, loved to keep them shut even when I wasn't sleeping. She said she loved me even more when I slept because on several occasions I came up with a smiling countenance while sleeping. She said she couldn't imagine what was making me so happy at that very tender age.

Mother said she loved me very much because my delivery gave her the least problems ... no long labor, no bleeding, no complications. My birth, she said, inspired her to give nine more births after me, and we are all alive except one. In all, she had twelve children, and I was the third in line.

My mother said, as she tells me today, "Kwame, I have never forgotten the day of your circumcision and naming. The naming came first, of course. Your father had invited many friends and neighbors and, of course, a <u>wanzam</u> (the circumciser). When the elder, whom your dad had invited to perform the occasion, took you into his arms, you were full of cries and didn't stop until the man put the drops of water and alcohol on your tongue. He said, 'Kwame, here is water. When you see water, it's water. And here is alcohol. When you see alcohol, it's alcohol and nothing else. You should always speak the truth.'

"After that you started crying as if you anticipated what was coming. The wanzam was ready with his surgical instruments, and you were circumcised, which brought prolonged cries for another week when the wound began to heal. With all that noise, I loved you more and more. You grew into a very bouncing baby boy and I was certainly proud of you."

Mother said I used to cry a lot at night, and she was very patient with me as if she owed me a lot for bringing me into this world. She said throughout my infancy, I never sucked my thumb, but, however, sucked greedily at her breasts at every feeding.

She said she soon found an antidote to my crying because I never loved anything better than the pacifier. It was a good substitute for the breast, and it surely got me quiet any time I had it in my mouth. When I was about three months old, my mother said she wanted to give me a breast milk substitute, but she regretted that because I just wouldn't take any Lactogen or S.M.A. or anything, as if I could tell the actual differences between an infant formula and breast milk.

Mother said, after the fifth month, I never wet my bed again and this pleased her very much. By the end of the sixth month, she had given me almost all my immunizations. And I was never ever sick; and when I was sick at all with, say a fever, I always loved to take my medication even if it was bitter quinine.

She said she was glad to see me taking my first steps at seven months, quite fast for an average baby. She gave me all the necessary encouragement and attention, and, in no time, I wanted to run instead of toddle along. From the time I walked, I was into many things and once almost caused the boiling soup to pour over my face but for the timely intervention of my mother. I wonder how I would have looked now if that eventuality had happened. Thank God it didn't.

At around the age of two, I was beginning to be aware of myself in the world. I started walking barefoot from then, and in no time the soles of my feet were as thick and tough as leather itself. Actually, Father couldn't afford shoes for me, and I remember I got my first shoes at about thirteen, when I was in form one in secondary school.

I was so anxious to go to school that I got my father to sew me a school uniform of khaki shirt and khaki shorts with braces at age three (my picture at three tells me this). I never went to kindergarten, but I wore my uniform always until the age of six, when my dream was fulfilled. I can remember my very first day at school. I was still proud but rather anxious to do something, either play or study.

In spite of everything, I still managed to get into a fight. I fought like a lion kicking, slapping, and biting. The circumstances of the fight were these: some of my peers were already into playing soccer. I was watching the game nonchalantly, but wishing greatly that I would be invited into the game. I had stood there for close to fifteen minutes when the ball was kicked my way. I kicked the ball ahead of me and chased it. All the other boys were angry and also chasing me for not kicking the ball back to them. Upon reaching the ball, I kicked it ahead of me. This infuriated my friends even more for almost spoiling their game. One tall boy caught up with me and took a swing at me. I swung furiously back and kicked. The tall boy missed a step and fell flat on his face. As I knew I couldn't match the boy in a toe-to-toe fight, I kicked him and ran as fast as I could. I was heading home. Home was just across the street from school. Mother couldn't understand why I had run home my very first day.

"What is it, Kwame? Why are you home so soon?"

"The teacher wants to beat me. That's why." I lied.

"You shouldn't be afraid of the teacher's cane. Come on. Let's go back."

"No."

"If you don't come along with me, you're rather going to get it from me."

"Mama, let me explain. Actually, the teacher is not after me, but some students want to beat me up. That is why I am here. Please don't send me back."

"You have to be tough, otherwise you can't go to school."

"I am tough because I just beat up somebody, and he is after me too."

Mother took me to my classroom, and had a talk with the teacher who, in turn, told the class not to frighten anybody off, after all, it was everybody's first day.

I had lost the half penny mother gave me. As a result, I was quite hungry the rest of the school time, as we did not go out for anymore recreation or recess and we closed at four o'clock in the afternoon. No sooner had we closed when I was in the midst of another brawl. This time I wasn't so lucky and I went home with a bruised shin which I never said anything about to Mother or Father because I knew they would give me some lashes as both Mother and Father never spared the cane.

I loved school despite my disappointing first day, and it soon became apparent that I was learning easily. My class one teacher really encouraged us and gave us much incentive for good behavior and learning ability. I remember, once, our teacher told us to sit with our legs crossed under our desks. No one remembered that day and when the teacher inspected us, I was the only one with my legs crossed. I got a leaf full of thuppence rice from Mame Fati. It was the teacher's reward for remembering.

By the end of my first academic year, I could read my English and the local language books well. I had to know how to read, because in class two there was a teacher everybody feared for her no-nonsense attitude. Mrs. Oduro, who was also the head teacher, was so severe that children dropped out of school after the first year. She always used the cane which wreaked havoc behind our backs and our legs. We terribly feared Mrs. Oduro, but she never had the chance to give me a thrashing because I was always well behaved and academically alert.

We all looked forward to recreation or recess because we could always kick the soccer ball around. Our girls also learned and played <u>aso</u> and <u>ampe</u>

well. Occasionally, they got the chance to practice netball with Mrs. Oduro, who although was severe, had a heart for training little girls. One thing I hated most about Mrs. Oduro was that she made doughnuts and toffees and sold them on credit to us little kids so that every morning after assembly, she collected the monies we owed her and we had nothing for the rest of the day. Our monies had been given us to buy rice and beans or <u>kokonte</u> and ground nut soup which were more filling than the doughnuts and the toffees. From this business, Mrs. Oduro was able to build a nice house, quite interesting for an elementary school teacher who are not paid well. Actually, she was very enterprising and seemed to have a real business acumen.

At the end of the third term in class two, Mrs. Oduro collected three pence from every boy and girl and used the money to organize a tea and bread party for her class. As much as I feared her canes, she instilled in me hard work and discipline. I believe I can attribute my beautiful handwriting (I hope I am not boasting) to her ever vigilant care.

It was she who gave me a first attempt to be a leader because after the first terminal examination, I was on top of my class so I got a chance to be a class prefect. I soon realized that being a class prefect meant a lot as the big students wanted to beat me up always after I had written their names for Mrs. Oduro's quick ones (we called her lashes). Despite their threats, I was not going to be intimidated by anyone. I got beaten up once or twice; but after, unrelentlessly, writing their names and with the full support of Mrs. Oduro, the bigger boys gradually became afraid of me, and I had full control of the class.

Religion formed an integral part of our education. Our school was Catholic. (St. Paul's Roman Catholic Primary School). We were made to start catechism quite early. We had to attend mass every Sunday and Wednesday. It was a must to do so because if one was caught absent, then, his five lashes of the cane would be waiting for him the following day.

At that time, mass was said in Latin, and we didn't understand a word of it. However, I loved and learned, enthusiastically, most of the Latin hymns of the church. I was always fascinated about the day I would receive the Holy Communion. There were tales and tales about the body of Christ. Some of the tales said that if you received communion without having gone to confession, then you would have a headache immediately. Others said that communion must not be chewed. If one did, his mouth would be oozing with blood.

We were made to hold the holiness of the sacrament in awe, and we never ate or drank even water on Sundays and Wednesdays until after one had received communion.

On Fridays, one really had to watch what he ate because we were not supposed to eat meat, not even the sauce prepared with meat. On this day, therefore, I made sure I went for my gari and beans. Most of all, these strict rules in the Catholic Church have since been abandoned. We now say Mass in vernacular, and we even use the drum as well.

Chapter VI

Elementary and Secondary School Days

As much as we were religious, we were also very superstitious and thought that juju or voodoo (bad medicine) worked.

I remember once in class five I was supposed to be in charge of the juju or voodoo before our football game with class six the following day. When I consulted some senior students about this, they instructed me to catch a toad. I was supposed to give the toad as much alcohol as I could and put a lighted cigarette in its mouth. After that I should put the poor toad in a cigarette tin, put a lid on it, and bury it in the center of the school field.

I had already written the names of all the eleven players in class six on a piece of paper, folded it, and inserted it into the mouth of the toad. Poor toad indeed. I buried it in the night when the night watchman would not catch me.

The next day, I instructed my teammates that no one should urinate on the field prior to the game, as that would spoil the juju. At three o'clock in the afternoon, our match started. Our girls cheered like mad as the match wore on. In less than thirty minutes, we were down by three goals. Surely, my juju was not working. We managed to score one goal but in the end, we were beaten by four goals to one. From then onwards, I had reason not to believe in juju because mine didn't work, but I was always haunted and fascinated by it.

At that age, I got to know that juju could bring a person money. The people called it sika duro, or money medicine. I was told if there was a rich man who always had his head shaven, then one knew that he was using his hair for juju for money. I was even told that sometimes a man could sacrifice potency of his sexual organ for medicine for money. We need money, but why should the love of money overtake our own sound reasons? And the love of money had drawn people to indulge in ritual murders. The case and murder of Kofi Kyinto was an example.

Superstition was at its peak for me when I was going to take my Common Entrance Examination. I wished highly to get juju to help me with the examination. I took no chances and studied hard; however, Charles, my friend, came up with something:

"Kwame, do you want to top the whole country in this year's examinations?"

"Yes, I wish I could," I said and smiled. Charles knew me to be a good student but he still said, "I know where we can get blessed Indian ink for our exam."

"What is that supposed to do?"

"It will help you write correct answers only, plus it will help you to write a lot faster."

"How can we get the Indian ink for our fountain pens then?"

"I know a certain man at Amakom in Kumasi who will do everything for us."

Charles, actually, took me to the man the next day. The fetish priest asked us to meet him at the Tafo Cemetery that evening, and we did. There, ritual after ritual was performed. The man demanded some cedis, and to my utter surprise, Charles produced the money. Where did he get this sum of money? I later realized that Charles had stolen it. As we were far away from our houses and also in the cemetery, I was caught with an unimaginable fear and wished I had not come along at all.

I was trembling with fear and started to cry. The fetish priest consoled me and said things would be fine and finished soon. After he performed his last ritual, which consisted of the sacrificing of the white hen he brought along, he brought us back to Amakom and advised us not to mention anything about the night's episode. Charles was very excited because he knew he was going to top the exam with me.

We took our exam a week after Kwame Nkrumah had been deposed. As young as I was, I couldn't believe a ruler of Nkrumah's caliber could be deposed but, surely, he was; on account of the country's first coup d'etat in 1966. There was excitement everywhere in the country.

All the pupils from St. Paul's Elementary got to Prempeh College where we were bullied by the seniors at the college. After our bullying, we additionally faced a tough examination, and we all complained. If I had depended only on the supposed ability of my fountain pen with its Indian ink to try to succeed in the exam, I would have failed.

When the results finally came, both Charles and myself had passed but we weren't the top students in the country. I got admitted to my first choice secondary school, St. Augustine's College. My father was very instrumental in seeing that I really got admission because he traveled from Kumasi to Cape Coast to check up. My father had not even gotten his form four leaving certificate, but he saw that if his children were to achieve anything, it would be through education, so he really gave me the encouragement.

He bought the items on my prospectus after I had passed the interview conducted by the then headmaster of St. Augustine's, Mr. Oppong. I was my father's first child to go to a boarding school, and in far away Cape Coat, so he tried his best to give me all the provisions and a big enough amount for pocket money.

"Kwame, this is a dream come true for me. Do your best at the secondary school."

"Papa, I won't let all your money and efforts go to waste. With God's help, I will really study to be somebody in future."

"What will you like to be in future?"

"I want to be a teacher because Kwame Nkrumah, our deposed president, and most of his ministers were teachers."

"You could try harder to be a doctor. What do you say to that?"

"Every father wants his son to be either a doctor or a lawyer, but who will teach all these people? I think I would like to be a teacher of all these professionals."

"If you want to achieve something, Kwame, go for the gold. Try to be the top, so that if in the process you don't get the gold, you might at least settle for silver. Don't take anything lower. I say be a doctor."

My mother who had been in the kitchen, finally came to the room with Father's lunch and joined in the conversation and said, "Ei Kwame, you are a lucky boy; you will be going to college in a week's time. You know I didn't go to school, but I've grown to realize the importance of education. Study hard. Will you?"

"Yes, Mama, really, don't worry about me much because you know my performance in school. I don't joke with my studies."

"Over there, all the students will be the top in their previous elementary schools, so it isn't going to be easy," Mother said. "The best students in the country are selected to go to St. Augustine's College."

"Just pray for me because, Mother and Father, I will come home next term as the first student in my class. I'm sure of that."

"Respect your teachers because they are going to shape your life for the future." Father said.

"And don't eat too much. Don't fight over food to disgrace us."

"Oh, Mother, how can I disgrace you? We don't have a lot of money, but we do have high self-esteem. You've brought us up to respect ourselves and I thank you for that."

As the week drew to its close, I was very anxious to travel away from home for the first time. However too, I was afraid because I had heard much about "homoing" or hazing of new students.

On the bright morning of September 6, 1966, my father and mother got me to the lorry station and gave the keys of my trunk and chop box to me and advised me to keep them well and not be careless. Mother had wanted to accompany me to Cape Coast, but she handed me over to some senior students whom she found to be well behaved.

No sooner had Mother departed than the seniors started with the bullying. The trick of the seniors that I remember most was the "Fill in the Gap." A senior student will take the nose of a new student between his fore and middle fingers and snap it hard to cause a lot of pain to the nose.

I played a trick on one mean senior and blew my nose in his hand. Unfortunately, he did not have a handkerchief so he just wiped the mess on my shirt which I thought was very wicked because it was my newest white shirt.

The lorry, finally, made its way out of Asafo Market after the "aplankes," or touts, had loaded our trunks and chop boxes on top of the lorry. Since all the passengers were students, the seniors, all of a sudden, caused the new students to sing their hearts out. We were asked in turn to tell stories. If one couldn't tell a good story, he got a knock on the head or he filled in the gap. All the disciplining of the new students made us tougher before we came to the secondary school campus.

The journey was long. We passed through thick forests, scarps, and lowlands. Finally, I saw the sea for the first time and I was really excited. I could not wait to get on to the seashore. There was a lot of "homoing" on the first day, but I was not crying because I had been used to the bullying of the seniors.

It was a real sight when the first bell of the day went for supper. All the new students of St. John's dormitory were lined up and given instructions as if we were in the military, and we marched to the school's big dining hall. There, in the dining hall, students from other dormitories were doing sit-ups, filling in the gap, telling meaningless stories and crying. They were not as tough as I was, because I took all the bullying as if I was a man. My ability to clown and crack jokes saved me most of the time because I always got the seniors laughing. I also had a song of Bob Cole's and, surprisingly, all the seniors wanted to hear me sing that song over and over. The song was "Ketsew Oda Dua Do" or "The Lizard on the Tree." Thanks to Bob Cole for making that song because it saved me from too much bullying.

Since it was my first time of using the fork and knife to eat rice and stew, I was not doing too well with the cutlery. A senior offered to teach me how, and in the process ate half of my food. I was hungry, but I couldn't say a word. I had to go back to the dormitory and do some liquid soaking which consisted of soaked gari, sugar and milk. I was worn out to the bone after the long journey and bullying, so it was with gladness that the bell for lights out went.

The following day, all the students went across the street to the seashore in front of the school. We were supposed to make brooms from the coconut fronds. Those who could climb the tall trees were already cutting the huge leaves and also bringing down a lot of fruit.

Unaware of the energy and force of the waves, I went too close to the edge of the water and a huge wave broke on the shore. Before I could run away from the wave, I was covered by it and pulled into the sea. I did not know how to swim and was panicking. Really, I was drowning. Fortunately, some seniors from Cape Coast saw me in frantic efforts to get out of the water. They swam quickly towards me and rescued me. They gave me first aid and immediately took me to the school clinic.

That episode brought me some friends, for Francis and Joe became close and reliable friends until they themselves finished school. I cherished their friendship because they came from rich homes. Francis' father had been a minister in the deposed government so he was close to Kwame Nkrumah. Francis used to tell me a lot about what happened when the 1966 coup d'etat came.

He got to like me so much that he protected me, most of the time, from the bullying by the other senior students.

Classes started briskly the following Monday. Incidentally, I was in the same freshman class with Totobi Quakye and Dr. Kwesi Nduom, formerly Kwesi Yorke. We had teachers from almost every part of the world. There were teachers from Canada, England, India, Pakistan, and America. There was no doubt that our gatherings on St. Augustine's campus in 1966 were quite cosmopolitan. All this added to the beauty of the college. The white administration building was reminiscent of ancient Greek architecture with its white marble columns. The administration block also housed the staff common room and the church. There were big plots of land in front of the building and ferns and hibiscus flowers adorned the well-mowed carpet of grass.

Form One had four streams of A, B, C, D. One day, our literature master, Mr. Martin Owusu, came and announced in my class form one B.

"We are going to stage plays this term."

Since I was a bit assertive, I asked, "What plays are we going to stage, sir?"

"Shakespeare's and the Trojan War. The whole form will act Hamlet, Julius Caesar, and the Trojan War."

We had never heard of anyone like Shakespeare. However, we had heard bits about the Trojan War and the Wooden Horse in history class in elementary school, and I was lucky my class was to perform the Trojan War.

Mr. Martin Owusu was a good director, even though he was just out of a diploma college. He gave me the part of Agamemnon, and I remember this part very well because at the play's first staging, I forgot my lines and almost ruined the play, had it not been for another friend who prompted me.

"You had stage fright, Kwame," said Mr. Owusu.

"Yes, sir. It was my first time of being in front of so many people."

"We are taking the plays to other schools, so you must get your lines straight."

"Sir, it's not that I don't know my lines. I just panicked."

"I am going to change your part. Do you agree?"

"No, sir, I don't. I will really overcome my stage fright."

Mr. Martin Owusu gave me another chance, and I did so marvelously well at Holy Child Secondary School that I even won the heart of a beautiful young girl.

After the plays, the term was getting to its end. Homoing had slackened, and everybody was serious and concentrating on their books. The examinations for the first term were very important because the results would count at the Speech and Prize-Giving Day the following term. I studied hard and, luckily, when the term's results finally came to my father during the vacation, I was first in my class.

"Kwame, you had a good report. Apart from being the overall first student, you also topped in four subjects."

"I know I topped in Latin, but what are the other subjects?' I asked.

"You topped in French, Literature, and English Language."

"What about General Science and Mathematics, since you want me to become a doctor?"

"You didn't do too badly there, either. I think I will have a doctor someday."

"Let's hope so, Papa. I have won five prizes for being first and tops in four subjects. What are you going to give me for my effort?"

"I will buy you a kente cloth."

"Really? Wonderful," I said, and bowed and touched my father's feet in reverence.

"If you continue like this, you'll always have presents from me."

"Thank you, Papa. I will do my best." During that Christmas, father slaughtered a sheep to celebrate the festivities and also being first in class. I was really becoming my father's favorite child and I could see he was really proud of me. This was even more evident when he increased my pocket money for the second term.

"Write to me when you get there because I want to be there at your Speech and Prize Giving Day to see you receive your prizes."

"I will do that. I am really excited and your presence will add to the serenity of the occasion."

Before I left for Cape Coast in January, Mother spent two days preparing me <u>sheto</u>, or stewed red peppers, for my "solid soaking" of gari. Mother bought me gari, twelve tins of milk, a dozen sardine tins, and two tins of corned beef. These provisions were what the Ghanaian students called, "Essential Commodities."

"Mother, why all these provisions?"

"Just to make you study harder. I didn't go to school, but I know studying is hard and needs everything to make it easier for you. That is the reason for all the provisions."

"Aren't you pampering me too much?"

"Not my future doctor, Kwame," Mother said with a warm smile.

"Thanks, Mama. I will always study hard to make you happy."

"Okay. You should never forget to try your hardest."

Chapter VII

Speech and Prize Giving Ceremonies of 1967

I went back to St. Augustine's College for the second term. The term was an interesting one since we were going to have our Speech and Prize-Giving Day. The first year students had a busy time ahead of them, for it was upon their shoulders that lay the cleaning of the school compound. We were all givens cutlasses to cut the grass of the school. All the trees were pruned by us. We painted some of the school blocks and cleaned the toilets and bath houses, and replaced the "shankometers" (toilet papers).

After a couple of weeks of such activity, we were all by the seashore cutting down coconut leaves with which to build a platform and a shed on the quadrangle in the center of the school compound. Every day after classes, we would go to the beach and work hard in spite of the fact that we swam, climbed the coconut trees, and plucked some fruit to enjoy.

As we came back to campus, I organized my class into groups of ten, and each group had something to do. We worked hard and sang in accompaniment. Pretty soon the work was enjoyable and we finished in record time. Our teachers praised us for a job well done.

The Speech and Prize-Giving Day was slated for the middle of the term, and it soon closed in upon us. In the interim, all the students in the school (900 of us) had been busy practicing cultural drumming and dancing. Each tribe brought its culture to a focus. The Ashantis practiced Adowa and Kete and the Fantis practiced the Adenkum and the Apatampa. The Northerners practiced their high stepping dances and the Ewe and Gas practiced the Agbadza and Kpanlogo respectively.

I am a Fanti but I chose to be with the Northerners since I was fascinated with their energetic and aggressive dance.

On February 20th, under a blue sky spotted with cottony clouds and a warm sunshine, we had the Speech Day. The headmaster, Mr. Seddoh, had invited the American ambassador to be our guest speaker. All the members of staff, in their academic gowns, were seated to the left of the platform and all, except, the headmaster and the smartly dressed form one students were seated. A waft of cool breeze from the Atlantic Ocean blew intermittently to cool our sweaty pores.

The form one students and the headmaster were in front of the school entrance to meet the American ambassador and usher him to the quadrangle.

When he arrived in his white Cadillac, he was met by the headmaster and we all cheered and applauded the ambassador. He was dressed in a navy-blue suit with a blue and white polka-dot tie. He was tall and broad shouldered and had a slow but gentle gait. He waved and said, "Hi," to us. We all turned around and sang a well-practiced Fanti song in welcome. When we reached the quadrangle, the members of staff and the rest of the students, who had been waiting patiently, stood up until the American ambassador and the headmaster took their seats.

I still hadn't seen my father. He promised to come, but I was surprised of his absence so far. I kept looking. As I was almost doubting his presence, I saw a taxi pull up by the school notice board. I kept looking. The door opened and yes, it was my father. I made the sign of the cross to thank the gracious God for my father's presence.   The event was started with opening prayers by our Dutch school chaplain, Father Van Velzen. After that, the headmaster introduced the ambassador and other important guests. Soon after that, the ambassador was to give his address. He spoke distinctly, taking pains to enunciate correctly. He was formal. He spoke about the good relations between Ghana and the United States, the aid that the United States was giving the country, the Peace Corps' effort in the country, and the relation between sports and academic work. He pointed to the fact that the United States was ready to offer scholarships to deserving students in both the academic and sporting disciplines.

"There is the American Field Service, and a student who performs well is sure to be in the United States for one year," he pointed out.

We all applauded. The ambassador ended his speech and donated six thousand cedis towards a scholarship fund and gave a number of books for prizes to the students.

When the headmaster gave his speech, he elaborated on academic excellence and referred to the past year's results which were the best in the country. He said discipline was the backbone of every ambitious endeavor, and therefore urged the students to be both disciplined, not only at school, but also at home with our parents. He touched on the excellent sporting record of our school, and urged the athletes to train very hard for the impending inter-college athletic competition of all Cape Coast and other Central Region schools right on St. Augustine's Sporting Field. The long speech, intermittently punctuated by applause, finally came to an end with a strong admonition to the students to study very hard and reach for higher heights.

The school's senior prefect also spoke and recounted on the school's academic, sporting, and disciplinary efforts of the past year. He praised the teaching staff and students for their mutual cooperation and wished that the confidence instilled in the students by the staff and headmaster would continue.

After the prefect's speech, it was prize-giving time. I was the first to be called upon to get a prize since I was first in my class and also first in four subjects. My book collection that day included The Adventures of Huckleberry Finn, Man Eaters of Kumaon, Le Rouge et Le Noir, and Chaucer's Pardoner's Tale.

Someone in form three, called Maurice Brunner, collected eight prizes in his class. He was very much applauded.

After the Prize-Giving ceremony, the headmaster thanked the representatives of Pioneer Tobacco Company, Valco, and the American ambassador for donating books to deserving students. The event was ended with closing remarks and a prayer by the school chaplain once again. The headmaster in a loud bellow shouted our school motto:

"Omnia Vincit Labor!" (Labor or hard work conquers everything)

"Hurray!"

"Omnia Vincit Labor!"

"Hurray!"

"Omnia Vincit Labor!"

"Hurray!"

The students dispersed to meet their parents after a procession by the headmaster, the American ambassador, and staff had walked towards the white-columned administration building.

However, that was not it for the day. The night patiently awaited the much anticipated Cultural Drumming, and Dancing. Before the bell tolled for supper, the school prefects organized the forms one and two students to set the scene for the cultural activity. We brought benches from the Dining Hall after we had eaten. It was after this period that I had the chance to talk to my father who had been waiting patiently at the school's guest room.

"Hello, Kwame, I was proud of you."

"Thank you, Papa."

"I'll buy you a bottle of Coca-Cola to celebrate your success. How's that?"

"Oh, that'll be fine. Thanks."

My father led me to the guest room, his right arm on my shoulders. I introduced my father to some of my friends, and I could see my father was very elated indeed. As we got to the guest room and father got our refreshments, he said, "Your mother and brothers and sisters bring greetings from Kumasi. I brought you <u>sheto</u>, gari, and bread from your mother. Everyone is well at home."

"Gee, thank her for me. You really love and care about me and I certainly appreciate all your efforts."

"We do that to encourage you to study hard to be somebody in future."

"I'll do my utmost best, Papa."

"I have also almost finished paying all the installments on your kente cloth, and the cloth weaver said it will be ready by the time you come home for the holidays."

"I'll love to have my own kente. Indeed some of the students already have kente, and they really show off a lot."

"Cultural drumming and dancing is on your program for tonight. Are you going to take part or you will only be a spectator like me?"

"Oh, no, I am taking part. I joined the Northerners and we've been practicing since school started this term. Yakubu, our leader from Tamale, is a wonderful drummer and you should look forward to a good night of cultural diversity from all the tribal groups."

"Is it a competition among the tribes really?"

"Yes, Papa. There will be a fine prize for the tribe that will be judged the best."

As my father and I talked on, the bell in the school tower was ringing. I led my father to his seat and quickly went and changed clothes into tribal gear at St. John's dormitory and joined my group. Ubiquitous sounds of drums permeated the evening's atmosphere. When all the invited guests were seated, the headmaster gave a brief synopsis of the event and the Ashantis were called upon for their show. The adowa dance was first and the boys were very elegant with their dance steps. The drumming was melodious and after a twenty-minute interval, it was the turn of the Fantis to drum and dance. Their adenkum, apatampa, and Asafo songs thrilled everyone present. Of course, most of the spectators were Fantis and it looked as if they were sure to win the coveted prize. But the Gas came up with a wonderful display of dance and drumming to the kpanlogo and they, too, were sure to win.

Then, the heavy, melancholy sounds from the Ewe tall drums sounded for the agbadga. It was a really vigorous dance of the arms and the upper body. Two rows of five dancers each shuffled and wiggled to the center of the dance area. The headmaster, an Ewe himself, was so enthused about the tribal rhythm of drum and dance that he joined his tribe and put on a real dance show. His wife couldn't sit and she too joined. We all applauded and cheered wildly for our favorite head and his wife. After the dance came to an end, the dancers, the headmaster included, were beaded with sweat.

The Northerners took the stage. I was behind Yakubu. With an hour-glass drum under his armpits, he sent us jumping high and kicking into the charged atmosphere. Our dance steps, aggressive as they were, received the most applause, but we didn't win the prize as everyone thought. The Fantis were first and there was a joyous commotion for them. I think the judges were biased. The prizes were given to the overall best tribe and Yakubu was adjudged the best drummer and dancer.

I met my father again who couldn't wait to congratulate me.

"You did marvelous."

"Thanks."

"I was really watching you. I thought either the Gas or the Northerners should have been the first prize winners."

"I thought so too, but we weren't the judges."

"Kwame, it's late, and I must get going."

"When will you go to Kumasi?"

"Tomorrow, of course. You know I have to go to work on Monday."

"Where do you put up tonight then?"

"Don't worry. I know some people in town."

"Okay. I will see you off at the school gate by the Cape Coast Hospital."

"Sure. Thanks."

We walked past the administration building towards the hospital. My father didn't own a car so he took a taxi after he had given me a bear hug and three cedis. I thanked him because I was a very rich man indeed with three cedis in my pocket.

Seated in the front seat of the taxi, my father said, "I'll tell all I saw to your mother and brothers and sisters."

"Okay, Papa, and good-bye."

He waved, and I waved back and looked in the taxi's direction until it vanished into the velvety black night. I turned around and felt a pound of happiness weigh on me. I was a lucky boy to have such a mother and father. They cared a lot, and to me that was all that mattered. As the bell was tolling for lights out, I hurried to my dormitory. I had just enough time to take a shower, went under my mosquito net, and curled up in bed. I said a prayer to thank the Almighty for a really blessed and happy day. Soon, I dozed into the night which had been cooled by the constant breezes of the Atlantic and I was in happy slumber land.

It was a good night's sleep full of pleasant dreams of the day before. I slept so well that I found it difficult to wake up at five in the morning. The Harmattan chill was really felt, but it didn't bother me too much as I took my usual morning cold shower. It was a Sunday, and after breakfast, all the students went to the chapel for the Catholic service.

Father Van Velzen gave an elaborate sermon with fervid eloquence. He advised us to be morally good and take our studies seriously. He was happy to see many students go to communion. We sang sacred hymns to a piano accompaniment; and after the service, I went to the dormitory for my books and went to the library. All was quiet, except for the roaring of the sea and a fisherman's song on the beach when they were pulling in the day's haul of fish.

The day's quiet aura contrasted with the noise and activity of the day before. It was good for studying. I studied for many long hours and only stopped when the bell went for lunch.

Seniors Francis and Joe saw me. They wanted me to do some washing for them in the afternoon so I obliged and washed their trousers, shorts, shirts and bed sheets for them. They paid me back with gari, sheto, and corned beef "soaking." I relished the taste.

Chapter VIII

Sports and Academics at St. Augustine's: 1967

The school and college's athletic competition was the dream event of every student in Cape Coast. St. Augustine's was a force to reckon with in the Central Region, but our rivals, Adisadel College and Mfantsipim, were also training hard according to our sports master, who was also our coach.

I was too little to create any impact in sports. However, in form three, there was a national athlete by the name of George Daniels. Everyone was looking forward to seeing this athlete, much heard of in Cape Coast. He was a sprinter and a little bowlegged. He was tall as well as muscular and very soft-spoken. He also happened to be a Fanti, my tribesman.

Students of St. Augustine's trained very hard. Every morning, at about four thirty, the sports master, Mr. Tsiquaye, will go around every dormitory to wake up the athletes for training. He was a stern disciplinarian and he always came with cold water and a cane. First, he would come to your bed and try to wake you up. If students proved a bit difficult, then he would sprinkle the cold water on them and leave. But woe betide anyone if he came back and you weren't awake and ready with your training gear, then you'd be in for some quick lashes! He instilled so much fear in the students that everyone did quickly as he commanded. He was a real military man. I wasn't one of the athletes, but Francis, our school shotputter, told me that they had to run along the sandy beach for some time and then do road work along the Cape Coast, Takoradi trunk road.

"We ran towards Cape Coast University, where we really train hard on the hilly terrain. It's difficult work," he said.

"I can imagine that, but I think it helps you. You have good bulging muscles."

"Yes, I hope to win first place in this year's shot-putt and perhaps compete for the nation."

"Sure, you can do it. I will root for you."

"You better or I'll really give it to you."

After training for about three weeks, the athletes were ready. As custom demanded, the headmaster and the sportsmaster made an appeal for funds. Every class prefect was to ensure that each student contributed something towards buying glucose, oranges, and tins of milk to refresh the athletes after their performance on the field. I collected my class' contribution after I had paid fifty pesewas. There were forty of us in my class and our total came up to ten cedis, which I handed over to the sports master at a morning assembly.

The much awaited days finally came. We, the boys of St. Augustine's, were sure to meet girls from the girls' schools of Wesley Girls High School and Holy Child Secondary School. Also, there were girls from Aggrey Memorial and Ghana National Schools, which were co-educational.

On those days, I put on my best white trousers and white shirt with black shoes to match. It was the only prescribed attire by the headmaster. I was sure to see Lily Ben Smith (may she rest in peace) also from Kumasi. She was attending Aggrey Memorial School. She was my classmate at St. Paul's Elementary and, as little as I was, I had a crush on her. Meeting her was the more reason why I looked so much forward to the athletic event.

On the 15th and 16th of March, the school was pulsating with vibrant student life. Students converged from all corners of Cape Coast. There was a march past by the athletes. Our students wore green and white track suits and the team was led by Francis, the captain. No one missed George Daniels because he was the tallest among the lot. Adisadel had a yellow and black track suit. Mfantsipim had an all white track suit. Aggrey Memorial was in their flaming red track suits and Ghana National had a black and white striped suit. The girls's schools were resplendent in white, blue, and red skirts and white tops.

There were songs of "samanmo" (cheerleading songs) everywhere on the field as different groups of students from individual schools sang on top of their voices to cheer their athletes on. The track judges and the starter, dressed in white, were all set for the competition to begin. First were the eliminations.

The hundred yards was the first event. George Daniels was in the second heat. The first heat was started well and a Ghana National student won it. The time came for the second heat and anxieties were high for St. Augustine's because of our dear George. The starter called them to the starter's line. There were eight students lined up.

"Ready," came the voice of the starter.

"On your marks."

"Get set."

He raised his gun into the air and the gun failed to fire. The athletes got off their lines and did some short practice sprints. The starter got his gun ready once again and called the athletes to their marks. All was quiet and everyone's attention was focused on the athletes.

"Ready."

"On your marks."

"Get set."

The athletes raised to the starting position and the gun blasted. A student from Adisadel shot in front as it seemed like George Daniels had had a bad start. In a good fifty yards, the Adisadel boy was leading, followed by an Mfantsipim student. George was in close third but, all of a sudden, after the fifty yard line, George burst out with fantastic acceleration. He caught up with the Mfantsipim student and madly chased the Adisadel athlete. By the eighty yard line, he and the Adisadel student were neck and neck. George passed the Adisadel student at the ninety yard line and coasted to a strong finish at the line. Applause was ubiquitous, and George was given a standing ovation. When his time for the event was reported by the announcer, George had equaled the Central Regional record set five years back.

St. Augustine's students sang <u>samanmo</u> songs and danced and taunted the Adisadel students. George won all his heats in the other events and anchored the one ten by four and two twenty by four events to a first place for St. Augustine's. The school was doing well in the field events also as Francis won the shot-putt easily and Baffoe-Bonnie, popularly known as Trickish, won the pole vault with entertaining and stylish acrobatic antics. The scoreboard showed us on top.

After the day's events, I made a mad dash towards the Aggrey Memorial stand. Sure enough, Lily, my crush, was there. In a coyish manner, I greeted her with a salute and offered my hand for a handshake. She obliged and smiled a white smile.

"How are you, Kwame?"

"I am fine, and you?"

"Alive and studying hard."

"Me too. I collected five prizes at our speech day. Why didn't you come when I wrote and invited you?"

"I had a test coming up so I decided to stay in school and study."

"Did you pass your test then?"

"Yes, I did. I wrote to Master Appiagyei, our elementary school head teacher, to inform him about my performance."

"I guess I should write to him, too. He'll be very proud. He was instrumental in getting my father to send me to secondary school."

"I like Master Appiagyei."

"I do too." I said.

"When do you go on vacation? We go in three weeks. In fact, we have exams right after the athletic competition," Lily said.

"We have about a month left so there's plenty of time," I said.

"Don't take any chances because you could be caught with a lot of work by the time exams come."

"Oh, I study all the time. My friends don't call me 'bookworm' for nothing."

As we talked and walked on, we got to the school gate where the Aggrey Memorial bus was standing. The driver honked the horn when he saw their school uniform. I wasn't looking forward to that because I was having a good time with Lily. She gave me a hug and hurried onto the bus.

"Bye, Kwame. See you tomorrow."

"Sure, there's tomorrow also for the finals." She blew me a kiss and the driver took off. I waved until the bus was no longer in sight. I got back to the dormitory to join my friends in an excited conversation over the day's events.

"Do you think we are going to be champions this year?" I asked senior Francis, who was still in his track suit and talking and gesticulating.

"We might, but it is not going to be easy. Adisadel boys are a real threat this year. We are only two points ahead of them."

"Well, as long as we have George Daniels, we shall, definitely, take the trophy. There's no doubt about that."

"Bravo for your confidence in the team, Kwame. Just keep your fingers crossed and say a prayer or two for us."

"I will."

Senior Francis led me to the dining hall where we were welcomed to a nice cuisine of our favorite rice and beans. Each student was given a boiled egg. On the athletes' table, their meals were richer and more sumptuous than the rest of the students'. In addition to the specially prepared meals, each athlete had two tall glasses of hot chocolate, a tin of milk, and some cookies. I was envious of all the care and attention given to the athletes, so I vowed to run for the school some day.

We slept soundly that night. I guess we were satisfied with our first place on the scoreboard. At five thirty in the morning, the bell sounded for "Wake Up." I had a bit of difficulty in waking up, but when I gathered that Mr. Tsiquaye had been around, I quickly grabbed my toilet bag and headed towards the communal bath house.

After I had attended church service, (it was the day for our dormitory to go to mass), I went to the dining hall for our usual Ajalo (a doughnut and a cup of hot chocolate). Classes began immediately after that.

At our daily morning assembly, the headmaster had announced that there would be only two classes for the day. The rest of the time would be used to prepare for the finals of the athletic competition. We, therefore, broke classes at nine twenty, went for our breakfast, and cleaned the school compound. Our American teachers, Brother Eduardo and Brother Chester, were to oversee the cleaning.

At eleven thirty, we had picked up garbage and swept the compound to a spic and span cleanliness. Students started arriving on the field. The atmospheric aura was permeated with samanmo songs and the roaring of the Atlantic. By about twelve thirty, the whole school was full of athletes, students and other spectators. All the students, both boys and girls, were smartly dressed in their uniforms.

Our headmaster, finally, got to the public announcement system and, in an instant, quelled the sing-song commotion of the students. He recounted the history of the Central Regional "Interco" and how the day's finals should be conducted in the most sportsmanlike manner. He equaled the definite semblance of sporting discipline to academic discipline and excellence.

After thanking all the coaches, officials, and judges, he took his seat and all was set for the day's events. Today's <u>samanmo</u> songs were louder than usual. Two Catholic schools were on top; we were one of them and Holy Child School was the other. I was very happy about that because it was apparent that should St. Augustine's and Holy Child carry the day in both the boys' and girls' events respectively, then there was definitely going to be a dance for both schools, and we would get to meet girls from Holy Child.

The day wore on and in the boys' events, it was a very close competition between St. Augustine's and its rivals, Adisadel, but God was on our side and we won by three points. Holy Child also beat Wesley Girls by ten points.

Trophies were distributed to deserving athletes and George Daniels was judged the best athlete. After the closing ceremonies, our celebration was to last deep into the night and over the weekend.

"We were invincible, senior Francis," I said when I met my friend.

"You better believe it we were!"

"How would you help me to get the autograph of George Daniels?"

"I can help you. George is a good friend of mine. Come on. Let's go to form three B."

When we got there, yes, George was busy with his books. Senior Francis introduced me, and George recognized me right away as he referred to my prizes at the Speech and Prize-Giving Day.

"I marveled at your running abilities."

"Oh, you did. I am not surprised."

"Don't be boastful, George. You must just thank the good Lord for being so kind to you."

"Well, Kwame is academically gifted, and I wish I was like him."

My head became twice its size when I heard Senior George say this.

"God knows whatever talents he apportions to every individual. Yours is in sports and you must be grateful."

"Yes, senior. I think you should."

"Look at me. I don't have anything, but I am thankful for even always breathing," said Francis.

"Come on , Francis. Don't kid yourself. You are good at sports and you are intelligent too," George said.

"True, senior Francis is all round. Senior, thank God always."

"Oh, never mind, I was only joking when I said that."

"Senior Francis, tell senior George why we are here."

"Yes, Kwame wanted your autograph, so here we are."

"I will kindly give it and thanks for appreciating me."

"You are very welcome."

I got George Daniels' autograph and still have it. I am very proud of that because George went on to become a national and international athlete who won many medals and trophies and competed all over the world for dear mother Ghana.

The term was coming to an end, so I studied hard and was very successful in all my examinations. At school, I did well in every subject except art. I just couldn't draw and I remember my art teacher, Mr. Amos, giving me a twenty-nine percent once. I always hated and will never forget him for that because that meant I had to get between ninety percent and a hundred in the other subjects to maintain my first position in class.

School vacated for the Easter holidays, and I returned to Kumasi, fully excited to meet friends from Opoku Ware Secondary School and see my loving parents and brothers and sisters once again.

Just as the Americans have turkey for Thanksgiving, we had chicken for Easter. It was a very delectable and relishing fufu and peanut butter soup. My mother, especially, gave me the best parts of the neck, wings, and feet; and I was a happy boy indeed.

My father was not a rich man, but there was never a day that he didn't have food on the table for everybody in the family. Parental and sibling support was one thing I never missed as a growing boy, and I gradually learned to appreciate the idea of family togetherness.

After the two-week Easter vacation was over, I returned to Cape Coast to begin the third term and put finishing touches to the 1966-67 academic year which had been so kind to me and had been very enjoyable.

At the end of the term were the promotion examinations and these alone could let one repeat a class if he was so unlucky to get a below fifty percent aggregate. But such worries were not mine, as I was always way above that mark. I tried, as much as possible, to help weaker students and that boosted and sharpened my own intellect.

Things went well academically for me at the promotion exams, and when my report came during the long vacations, I was first again and was going to be the prefect in the best class in form two - that was form two A. Such was a typical academic year in the life of a student at a boarding school in Ghana.

In form three, we had a little option to choose either Music, Greek, or Art. I chose to study Greek and found it challenging. In form three alone, we were taking as many as fifteen subjects including English, math, literature, all the sciences, (physics, chemistry, biology), Latin, Greek, geography, history, economics, business, e.t.c.

It was in form four that we had to choose a minimum of seven subjects or a maximum of nine to prepare and present to the G.C.E. or General Certificate of Examination (West Africa) ordinary level, in form five. My father insisted that I become a doctor some day so I took nine subjects which included physics, chemistry, biology, elementary mathematics, additional mathematics, English language, English literature, Latin, and French. It was also in form four that we had the opportunity to write exams to qualify for an American Field Service (A.F.S.) scholarship to study for one year in an American high school.

That year, in 1970, for some reason, I did not take part in the exam, but one Kwesi Yorke, now Dr. Kwesi Nduom did. (He is currently the Minister for Energy in the Kuffour regime). He passed and was in America the following academic year. When Kwesi returned from Milwaukee after his year in America, he was an instant celebrity. He showed us his color pictures, which we found very fascinating because every picture in Ghana at that time was black and white.

He told us of how he watched color television (our television was also black and white) and how he played basketball and American football in high school. What delighted us the most was his newly acquired American accent. Sometimes, he overdid his accent, but we did not mind since we held him in awe.

At the next intercollegiate atheletics, Kwesi Yorke was fantastic and we thought, at that time, that he had been using steroids or had been given what we called running-power vaccinations. I participated in sports in form four and was merely average in the four forty yards.

In form five, though, I took the American Field Service exam and won the international scholarship. That was the turning point in my life because in July of 1971, I found myself at an all white town of Alexandria, Minnesota.

I was among fourteen other students from Ghana who had made it. There were students from St. Augustine's, Wesley Girls, Achimota,

Tweneboa Kodua, and Konogo Odumasi. The rest were from Holy Child, Tamale Secondary, and Navrongo Secondary School.

I remember students like Selma Ramatu Alhassan, Mary Anne Addo, Joe Lartey, Jr., and Emmanuel Yamusah. We all relished our rare luck and opportunity and braced ourselves for an adventurous effort in a land much, much different from ours.

The Walter Salts are pictured with their sons Tom and the recently arrived AFS student from Ghana, who prefers to be called Kwamina.

AFS student arrives at Walter Salt home

Stephen Kwame Mends of Kumasi, Ghana arrived in New York on July 19 and is now at the Walter Salts, his home during the coming year in which he will be Jefferson High School's American Field Service student.

It took "Kwamina" 10 hours by plane to New York and 30 hours during the trip by bus which took him to Minnetonka where he was met by the Salt family.

Kwamina, (his name meaning boy born on Saturday) is a charming representative of his country. He speaks English fluently and is looking forward to learning more of the customs of this country.

His gifts to his American family included JOROMI shirts for Mr. Salt and Tom. Mrs. Salt is wearing the "Kon mu adze" which is worn by Ghanian women. In describing it,

Kwamina stated the words meant "something around the neck."

Kwamina is pictured wearing the traditional dress of his country, the "Kente," worn primarily for special occasions. It is with pleasure that Alexandrians welcome Kwamina to this vicinity.

Kwamina has spoken to many organizations. He is pictured holding some of the pictorial copy which he uses.

And with talent not adviseable, Kwame demonstrates opening a coke bottle with his teeth.

This is Kwamina AFS student of Alexandria

Wearing his native cloth, Kwame smiles amidst Minnesota snow while warmed by his VIKING cap.

"I wish they'd have taken a picture of me in the snowmobile suit and helmet I wore to the VIKING game," said Kwamina Mends, "For I'd have sent it back to my people because I looked like an astronaut!" Kwame, as the students call him, has noted quite a change from the weather in his country of Ghana, West Africa, where the temperature ranges consistently from 72 degrees to 85 degrees. He couldn't imagine what winter would be like in Minnesota, but he has learned that if it's 10 degrees above zero, in Minnesota the residents think it's warm. He likes the snow and the activities it brings and he's braved the elements to run 4 miles each weekend as he keeps in shape for the cross-country events in which he will participate come spring. Track is HIS sport, and he's good at it.

Kwame is attending Jefferson High School under the auspices of the AFS program. At this time of the year in his country, there will be posters throughout the school describing the program.

International Scholarships

This is to certify that

Mr. Stephen K. MENDS

was granted an Award for one year of
secondary school study and community
experience in the United States during the
academic year 1971-1972 and successfully
met the program's requirements academically
and personally, thus becoming a permanent
associate of this organization.

President

Secretary

Pictured left to right are Mary-Anne Addo, Woodward and Merlie Casem, Jackie Pivac, Laurits Hansen, Julie

NEW ARRIVALS

January 10 — Girl — Mr. and Mrs. Wm. Bahe, Brandon
January 12 — Boy — Mr. and Mrs. Larry Pederson, Fargo
January 13 — Girl — Mr. and Mrs. Allen Christopherson, Alexandria
January 13 — Boy — Mr. and Mrs. David Herberg, Alexandria
January 13, — Girl — Mr. und Mrs. Kelly Gunderson, Alexandria
January 13 — Boy — Mr. and Mrs. Evald Carlson, Garfield

Alexandria hosts foreign students

As has been the custom for many years, Alexandrians were hosts last weekend to foreign students who are residing in American homes of the surrounding area. The event was planned by the local American Field Service Club, its Board of Directors, and the Jefferson High School AFS Club and is made possible through financial assistance from the local organizations and businesses who are interested in the continuation of the program.

The 11 students, who were guests in local homes, spent a weekend filled with activity. On Friday they met with students of Jefferson High School at a joint meeting before visiting other Alexandria schools. The foreign students appeared on KCMT-TV on the "Welcome Inn" program. Before attending the basketball game and the festivities which followed, they were entertained at dinner at Central School by the AFS Club and the Board. Following the game, a party was given in their honor at the Richard Arvold home.

Among many other activities, the foreign students were guests of the Alexandria Chamber of Commerce as manager, Mr. Harvey Hammergren, opened the Runestone Museum for the students.

The following is a list of the students who spent the weekend in Alexandria, their countries, and the American families with whom they are residing during their stay in the United States under the American Field Service program: Mary-Anne Addo of Ghana, West Africa, at the Floyd Boline home in Golden

Harvey Hammergren, right, greets Alexandria's foreign student, Kwamina Mends and Matty Llosa of Peru as they toured the Runestone Museum on Saturday. "Kwame" resides with the Walter Salt family in Alexandria.

Valley; Jackie Pivac of Auckland, New Zealand, at the Daniel Johnson home in Dassel; Laurits Hansen of Denamrk, at the David Maas home in Canby; Julie Woodward of Australia, at the Don Gray home in Long Prairie; Merlie Casem of the Philippines, with the Ed Reddys of Breckenridge.

Roberto Cavichioli of Brazil is residing at the George Schuler home in Breckenridge; Rodney May of Australia is with the Elwood Sather family in Madison; Kenzi Karasaki of Japan resides with the Myron Sandbergs of Little Falls; Maria Eugenia Dallo of Argentina is with the Irving Jandt family of Wendell; and Matty Llosa of Peru is with the Joe Givens family of Dawson.

New TV series to feature sewing

Beginning January 25 on KCMT Channel 7 at 4:30 p.m. Ann Wilson, extension clothing specialist at Penn State University and Sarah Cox, clothing instructor at the University of Minnesota, will show you how to improve your sewing ability.

Pick up a SEW SMART enrollment blank at many of the fabric departments located throughout the county. Or write or call Connie Eldem Extension Home Economist, Courthouse Alexandria, phone 763-6077.

Enroll and receive a free study guide that gives additional information to the television lessons.

Pictured with Mrs. Robert Davis, center, (treasurer of the local AFS Board) are left to right: Roberto Cavichioli, Rodney May, Kenzi Karasaki and Maria Dallo.

You are always welcome in Alexandria

Individual Cardinals performing in state mee

PAUL DYKE
GOLF

BOB ANDERSON
TENNIS

RICH NOOLAND
TRACK

KWAME MENDS
TRACK

STEVE MAACK
TRACK

JACK GI
TRAC

Under My Hat

By ERC AGA

Our AFS son, Kwame, from Ghana has started his long trip back home. It all happened early Wednesday morning at Long Prairie where some 50 or more AFS students said goodbye to their American parents, brothers and sisters. And believe me, it was a wet occasion! Tears steadily fell as the good byes were said . . . and I'll admit I added a few. Kwame had promised no tears and sadness for the farewell . . . and he held up like a man . . . tho his lips quivered when he stepped on the bus . . . turned . . . and then gave us that last beautiful smile. So . . . comes an end to one of the most rewarding experiences our family has been through. Kwame now goes on a two-week tour of the East . . . then to Kennedy Airport to board the plane back to Ghana. At home, the AFS will arrange for a family meeting on arrival . . . then they will hold the students for two days of return indoctrination. This is very important, for as difficult as it is for the students to come here and change to our ways . . . it's twice as hard for them to return home and pick up where they left off a year ago. After two days of intensive orientation and training . . . then it's home for big family re-unions and the beginning of the long tales about their American experiences. So . . . the first part is over. We have definite plans to have Kwame back, for he wants to be a doctor. And we hope that after his mandatory two years at home, he'll be back as a student at the University of Minnesota.

We're hooked on the AFS bit now . . . for we feel it's one of the best things we have going for a better understanding among the nations of the world. You would, too, if you'd give it a try. Anyway, Kwame is gone. We miss him and love him very much. His beautiful black and white smile has made our lives more meaningful. But gee . . . parting is rough.

+ + +

+ + +

Lake Region Press
Alexandria, Minnesota

Page Two - A
Friday, July 7, 1972

KWAME MENDS won the 440 yard dash at the Region 6 track meet by diving accross the finish line. Just after hitting the tape above, Kwame stumbled and fell, but he had the first place medal. Kwame really ran his heart out in the race and had his best time of the year, 51 seconds.

wamina's mother, seated, is pictured with 3 sisters, a usin and a friend.

is is Kwamina's father, . Nicholas D. Mends.

When asked for measurements of the mouth-tasting addition to the soup which sounds so American, Kwame said: "They just don't measure things in Ghana."

While in Minnesota, Kwame is a member of the Walter Salt family. His American brother is Tom Salt, also a senior at Jefferson High School. His American sister, Jeri Lee (Mrs. Hillemeier of Olivia) recently gave birth to a baby, so Kwame has an American nephew.

Expressing gratitude for his family, his teachers and the American way of life, this has been a great experience for the 18-year old boy. He's acquiring a bit of the slang language to use on his friends at home just because they'll expect him "to have changed a little." When he leaves Alexandria, will go along. He'll have a written diary also, for he makes a carbon copy of each letter he writes home. As for AMERICAN FIELD SERVICE, there couldn't be a greater organization. "Where else," said Kwame, "would you find every continent represented in one town as they were in Alexandria during the recently sponsored AFS weekend. I'll never forget any of this year and some day I hope to return."

asons Kwamina hopes this can come his profession.
Kwamina finds American foods ailar to those of Ghana but eir preparation is different. For
ap, a recipe which follows and be made with American stitutions.

Cut a chicken in small pieces and cook till tender. Add tomatoes and other desired vegetables and boil. Mix peanut butter with water and pour into soup, stirring constantly. Boil about 30 minutes. When oil comes to top, the soup is completed.

A Valentine Special

Kwamina has spoken to many organizations. He is pictured holding some of the pictorial copy which he uses.

This is Kwamina AFS student of Alexandria

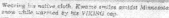

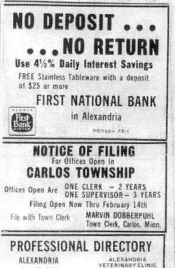

And with talent not adviseable, Kwame demonstrates opening a coke bottle with his teeth.

Wearing his native cloth, Kwame smiles amidst Minnesota snow while warmed by his VIKING cap.

"I wish they'd have taken a picture of me in the snowmobile suit and helmet I wore to the 'IKING game," said Kwamina Mends, "For I have sent it back to my people because I looked like an astronaut!" Kwame, as he students call him, has noted quite a change from the weather in his country of Ghana, West Africa, where the temperature ranges consistently from 72 degrees to 88 degrees. He couldn't imagine what winter would be like in Minnesota, but he has learned that if it's 10 degrees above zero, in Minnesota the residents think it's warm. He likes the snow and the activities it brings and he's braved the elements to run 4 miles each weekend as he keeps in shape for the cross-country events in which he will participate come spring. Track is HIS sport, and he's good at it.

Kwame is attending Jefferson High School under the auspices of the AFS program. At this time of the year in his country, there will be posters throughout the school describing the program.

"Everyone wants to come to the United States," said Kwame. It was only after winning an essay contest and being selected for an interview with the American Field Service Chapter in the capital, Accra, that he learned of his acceptance. His father is so proud of this opportunity which has come for Kwame for further ance of education is of primary importance in their land also.

Nicholas D. Mends, Kwame's father, is a farmer who raises cocoa. Most of the cocoa beans raised in Ghana are exported to the United States where they are processed to the baking ingredient. His mother, whose name is Araba, is a housewife and a trader in the Open Market where she prepares a delicacy of Ghana made with plantin (similar to bananas) which is mixed with flour and fried in palm oil. Kwame has 3 sisters and 3 brothers. The oldest brother is a draftsman; his oldest sister is married and has 2 children. The other children are still in school.

About 4 years ago, Kwame's parents were remarried in the Roman Catholic Church after a decision that native marriages were no longer recognized. His mother, once again a beautiful bride, wore a lovely white bridal gown with bouffant veil and carried a bouquet of mixed flowers.

Children's names in Ghana are chosen by the day of the week in which their birth occurs. His mother's name means "born on Tuesday." Kwamina means "born on Saturday." When asked what happened when more than one child in a family was born on the same day, Kwamina stated they added a number behind the name. Birthdays are never celebrated in Ghana, so the occasion of a birthday cake was a new experience. "On December ... they made a big deal out of is

said Happy Birthday over the intercom."

Kwame's first 9 years of schooling were at St. Paul's Catholic School. Education is compulsory in Ghana from the age of 6. There are two native languages spoken, TWI and FANTI. Most African languages, he said, are "tone" languages and many different things can be said while using practically the same words. If you wanted to write "Good Morning," for instance, it would be "me ma wo akye," similar in both TWI and FANTI. Kwame began his English in this school, continuing at St. Augustine's College which is similar to our high school. St. Augustine's also has 2 years of Junior College. With advances in grades being done by examination in Ghana, Kwame hopes he may complete his junior college program in only one year. If the possibility of a scholarship could arise, his greatest desire would be to come back to the United States to study medicine.

Kwamina comes from the city of KUMASI which has a population of 400,000 people. The city has AKOSOMBO DAM which supplies electricity to the city and surrounding territories. It has KUMASI FORT, originally built for protection of British soldiers against the ASHANTI tribes, but now a museum. There are government-owned industries: a shoe factory, a brewery, jute factories and a manufacturer of records. One can hear rhythm music in the city, for cultural drumming and dancing still has social significance; originally the drum was used to send messages from one tribe to another. The KENTE (native cloth) is still worn by both men and women for ceremonial and formal occasions. KUMASI has only one large hospital, CENTRAL, but smaller ones are scattered in the area. There are

Kwamina has spoken to many organizations. He is pictured holding some of the pictorial copy which he uses.

...nd with talent not adviseable, Kwame demonstrates... ...pening a coke bottle with his teeth.

This is Kwamina AFS student of Alexandria

Wearing his native cloth, Kwame smiles amidst Minnesota snow while warmed by his VIKING cap.

"I wish they'd have taken a ...cture of me in the snowmobile ...it and helmet I wore to the ...KING game," said Kwamina ...nds, "For I'd have sent it back ...my people because I looked ...e an astronaut." Kwame, as ...students call him, has noted ...te a change from the weather ...his country of Ghana, West ...rica, where the temperature ...ges consistently from 72 ...grees to 85 degrees. He ...dn't imagine what winter ...uld be like in Minnesota, but ...has learned that if it's 19 degrees above zero, in Minnesota the residents think it's warm. He likes the snow and the activities it brings and he's braved the elements to run 4 miles each weekend as he keeps in shape for the cross-country events in which he will participate come spring. Track is HIS sport, and he's good at it.

Kwamina is attending Jefferson High School under the auspices of the AFS program. At this time of the year in his country, there will be posters throughout the school describing the program.

"Everyone wants to come to the United States," said Kwame. It was only after winning an essay contest and being selected for an interview with the American Field Service Chapter in the capital, Accra, that he learned of his acceptance. His father is so proud of this opportunity which has come for Kwame for furtherance of education is of primary importance in their land also.

Nicholas D. Mends, Kwame's father, is a farmer who raises cocoa. Most of the cocoa beans raised in Ghana are exported to the United States where they are processed to the baking ingredient. His mother, whose name is Araba, is a housewife and a trader in the Open Market where she prepares a delicacy of Ghana made with plantin (similar to bananas) which is mixed with flour and fried in palm oil. Kwame has 3 sisters and 3 brothers. The oldest brother is a draftsman; his oldest sister is married and has 2 children. The other children are still in school.

About 4 years ago, Kwame's parents were remarried in the Roman Catholic Church after a decision that native marriages were no longer recognized. His mother, once again a beautiful bride, wore a lovely white bridal gown with bouffant veil and carried a bouquet of mixed flowers.

Children's names in Ghana are chosen by the day of the week in which their birth occurs. His mother's name means "born on Tuesday." Kwamina means "born on Saturday." When asked what happened when more than one child in a family was born on the same day, Kwamina stated they added a number behind the name. Birthdays are never celebrated in Ghana, so the occasion of birthday cake was a new experience. "On December ...

sang Happy Birthday over the intercom."

Kwame's first 8 years of schooling were at St. Paul's Catholic School. Education is compulsory in Ghana from the age of 6. There are two native languages spoken, TWI and FANTI. Most African languages, he said, are "tone" languages and many different things can be said while using practically the same words. If you wanted to write "Good Morning," for instance, it would be "me na wo akye," similar in both TWI and FANTI. Kwame began his English in this school, continuing at St. Augustine's College which is similar to our high school. St. Augustine's also has 2 years of Junior College. With advances in grades being done by examination in Ghana, Kwame hopes he may complete his junior college program in only one year. If the possibility of a scholarship could arise, his greatest desire would be to come back to the United States to study medicine.

Kwamina comes from the city of KUMASI which has a population of 488,900 people. The city has AKOSOMBO DAM which supplies electricity to the city and surrounding territories. It has KUMASI FORT, originally built for protection of British soldiers against the ASHANTI tribes, but now a museum. There are government-owned industries: a shoe factory, a brewery, jute factories and a manufacturer of records. One can hear rhythm music in the city, for cultural drumming and dancing still has social significance; originally the drum was used to send messages from one tribe to another. The KENTE (native cloth) is still worn by both men and women for ceremonial and formal occasions. KUMASI has only one large hospital, CENTRAL, but smaller ones are scattered in the area. There are

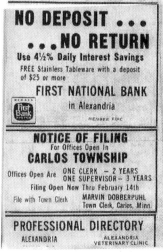

Chapter IX

International Scholarship (A.F.S.) and America, 1971

Immediately after I received word that I had been offered an international scholarship to study abroad, I wrote to my father who, in his next letter, was as excited as myself. Despite the fact that he was in a bit of financial crisis, he didn't fail to provide all the support a successful son could ask for, because we held going abroad, especially to America, as the biggest glory that could befall anybody, as we really marveled at the industrial, financial, and sporting prowess of this great democracy.

I got my first suit sewn for me by my father's tailor. My father bought me a suitcase (my first) and I packed my clothes, including a kente and native sandals and some gifts for my American host parents.

All the fourteen students were assembled in Accra for orientation, where we stayed with American expatriate families. These families introduced us to American food and deodorant. We were given a nationwide tour of interesting tourist attractions: Cape Coast and Elmina Castles, Akosombo Dam and the Adomi Bridge, Kumasi Cultural Centre, Bole and Paga Wildlife Reserves.

On July 19, 1971, we flew aboard a Pan Am Boeing on which were students from the whole African continent. There were students from Ethiopia, Uganda, Tanzania, the then Northern and Southern Rhodesia, and South Africa (they were all white students), and Liberia.

I was amazed and liked the cosmopolitan atmosphere on the plane. As we developed some engine problems, we had a longer-than-usual wait at the airport in Dakar, Senegal, before we flew directly to New York. For a novice at flying, it was a very long and enduring journey full of high expectations. The Big Apple, seen for the first time, was awesome. The skyscrapers of the New York skyline were ubiquitous. I couldn't believe my eyes. Was I mad? The architecture was the most exciting aspect of New York. Then we landed at John F. Kennedy Airport, and its enormity, cleanliness and beauty went beyond any description. What even amazed me beyond anything was that the whole airport, big as it was, was air conditioned. Amazing!

We were met at the airport by officials of American Field Service, who organized us and took us in long air-conditioned Greyhound buses and were off to C.W. Post College where we joined a cross-section of teenage students from all over the world. There were Japanese, Taiwanese, Burmese, students from Hong Kong, Australia, Argentina, Colombia, Brazil, and Chile. There were students from Iceland, Sweden, France, and Switzerland. They were from every corner of the world, and I had never dreamed of meeting teenagers from every part of the globe. This assembly gave me a degree of accomplishment at that tender age of seventeen. It did excite me indeed, and I couldn't wait to write home and to my friends at St. Augustine's about it.

Since America was just emerging out of the hippie era, we were given lectures on hard drugs, alcohol, and sex. We were warned not to be lax about ourselves to be drawn into such a mess by American students. We were asked not to drive for our own protection, and we were asked to portray our cultures to the American communities as best as we knew how. We had to always say "please" and "thanks" and "excuse me," and "I am sorry." I learned these simple courtesies, and today I know they are very helpful.

On the second day after our arrival at C.W. Post College, we boarded other Greyhound buses and were driven to our destinations. I was on the same bus with Mary Anne Addo, and we were headed for Minnetonka, a suburb of Minneapolis in Minnesota. It was a journey of almost a thousand miles, so one could imagine the time it took.

To me, the American landscape was beautiful. The roads and bridges were strong and well built. Occasionally, we saw rivers. The whole environment was richly green and the skies were azure and aqua blue.

There was even a toilet on the bus. To me to go to toilet on a moving bus was exciting and new. Mary Anne and myself punctuated conversation with sleep and trips to the toilet. After about thirty hours of travel, we were finally in the state of Sinclair Lewis and F. Scott Fitzgerald. Minnesota was beautiful and rustic. Lakes were ubiquitous and I saw the Mississippi River for the first time. I had learned much about this river in geography classes and Mark Twain's <u>Adventures of Huckleberry Finn</u> so I thanked God for discovering it myself.

At Minnetonka, host families had our names on placards. Mary Anne soon found her family, and the three-member family of Walt Salts met me and took me in their black Cadillac.

"Hi," they said.

"Hi. Pleased to meet you, Father and Mother."

"Call us Mom and Dad," Mrs. Salt said.

"How was your trip?" Tom Salt asked politely to start the conversation.

"It was long and tiring, but I saw some breathtaking landscape."

"Well, we still have about a hundred and fifty miles to go," Mom Salt added.

"Come on. Hop in the car, please. We shall have a very comfortable ride to Alexandria," Mr. Walt Salt (may he rest in peace) said.

"Thanks," I said.

I got in the very luxurious and comfortable car. Immediately, I found it was air-conditioned (the first time I had been in an air-conditioned car). Mr. Salt (Dad) got in the driver's seat and asked us to put on our seat belts. After driving a few miles, I could tell Dad was a very fine driver, but even then, for our own protection, he insisted on the seat belt.

"Tom, please, what is that metal ball in front of Dad?" I asked.

"Oh, it's a compass. You mean you never saw one like that before?"

"No."

"You will never get lost in this car," Mom Salt joked, and I acknowledged it with a white smile and they all smiled because of my ignorance.

"You must be hungry," Mom said.

"Yes, a bit, thanks."

"You want some hamburgers?" Tom asked.

"I've never eaten a hamburger before."

"Great, you should try it. You'll love it," Mom said.

"Yes, in America everybody likes hamburgers," Tom said.

Dad was always quiet, so Mom asked him to stop at a Burger King and soon we were at the joint. We took our seats at the very nice and immaculately clean restaurant, and Mom and Dad got the burgers while

Tom and I tried to carry on a conversation. We were both not nervous and I knew that Tom would be a good guy. When the victuals were brought, mom had bought me a deluxe hamburger and a milkshake.

"Here you go, Kwame. Enjoy your meal," she said.

"Thank you very much."

I liked the Burger King hamburgers immediately. It was nothing like my native fufu or ampesi or dokon, but it's exciting delicacy was enough to let me like it immensely.

"Do you like it?" Dad finally talked.

"Yes, Dad, very much."

"Good for you," Mom said.

"Mom, you should get him to try hot dogs also."

"Really, am I going to eat dogs?"

"No, Kwame. It's like a sausage between a bun," Tom tried to explain. I had to see a hot dog before I believed it.

Dad was smiling because of my lack of knowledge about American food, but I was not embarassed, only curious. As we finished our meal and got back to the car, Mom told me that she had been a teacher at her own private school.

"What did you teach, Mom?"

"I taught everything."

"You must be very intelligent to teach every subject."

"Thanks, I just tried my best for the students," Mom was being modest.

After we had strapped on our seat belts again, Dad took off slowly and drove along, occasionally stopped by red lights (we didn't have traffic lights in Ghana, so it was a new phenomenon for me). Finally, we were on the freeway, and slow speed gave way to instant acceleration. I looked at the speedometer and Dad was going fifty-five miles per hour.

I was tired, and in no time was dozing. My new family let me sleep. When I woke up, we were at Osakis.

"We have a short while to go yet." Dad said.

I was struck by the verdant coloration of the environment. What surprised me was that it was eight o'clock in the night, but the sun was still up, and everywhere was bright daylight. My country is on the equator, and almost after six P.M. it gets velvety, pitch black dark as the sun sets. By eight o'clock, it is absolutely dark, and most people are already in bed.

Soon, the green and white sign said "Alexandria." I was excited and tried to see almost everything at once. Dad drove on the main street, which was bordered on both sides by shops and restaurants. We stopped at a red light and I saw a police station on the left and a post office on the right. As we drove ahead, I saw a very enormous statue.

"What's that, Tom?"

"It's a statue of a Viking," Mom said.

"It's called 'Big Ole,'" Tom added.

Mom gave a brief historical overview of the warlike and travel-happy Vikings who, she claimed, were even in Minnesota from Sweden before Columbus discovered America. Big Ole was imposing. It was the statue of an impressive masculine figure in war gear, a spear, and a Viking helmet with the characteristic horns. I held the statue in awe.

We took the road to the left of Big Ole and soon I saw a lake, some geese, ducks, and some coots. After we passed the white gas tanks, we took a right and headed home. There were green fields of corn, alfalfa, wheat, and soybeans on both sides of the road. Dad went a little ways and slowed down. I saw a big wooden sign, "Walt Salt." He turned to the right off the road and we were at the Salts' house. The house was situated on one side of majestic Lake Darling. The sun was setting on the lake and a dazzling golden wake and coloration sang to the sunset.

"Welcome to our home, Kwame," Mom said.

"Thank you."

"Just feel at home here. If you need anything, ask me," she said.

Tom took my suitcase and said, "Kwame, your room is all made up in the basement. Come, let me show you."

I followed Tom down the stairs and he showed me a nice room with posters on the walls. I sat on the bed and felt its soft mattress and comfort. In Ghana, I slept on a mat on the cemented floor. Both floors had a soft, blue, shaggy carpet. The furniture was beautiful, as we had Davenports, rocking chairs, and stuffed chairs. After Tom showed me the toilet and the shower, we came up and Mom had laid the table and served hot dogs and milk in tall glasses. The taste of hot dogs was likable but the taste of fresh two percent milk was funny. Back home milk was for the rich people, and it came as evaporated milk (Carnation) in cans. To drink milk with a meal was new and exotic for me, but I liked the idea. We just had water (not even cold water because my parents never had a refrigerator). We had ahina, which had been smoked with palmnut fibres, and we always put a piece of camphor or mothball in the water.

I finished my supper and said goodnight to my new family and went to sleep in my room. I woke up early after a night of dreams. The sun was already up at about 5 A.M. I brushed my teeth and took a shower as I was used to doing every day in Ghana.

Mom was already up.

"Good morning, Kwame," she said.

"Good morning."

"Did you have a good night's sleep?"

"Yes, thanks."

"I'll fix breakfast."

"Okay, Mom."

I took the newspaper and tried to read. Their newspaper was a lot bigger than our <u>Daily Graphic</u> and <u>Ghanaian Times</u> and the <u>The Mirror</u>. I read for a while. I saw the cartoons and didn't understand them. I found Ann Landers to be very interesting. Dad and Tom were also up, and Mom was already ready with the scrambled eggs, bacon, toast, orange juice, and milk. At home I sometimes had <u>Kooko</u> (porridge) and bread for breakfast. If I was lucky, then I had rice and stew or gari and beans.

After breakfast, I took a good look at the house. I discovered there was a dishwasher and washing machine in the house. So I wasn't going to use my hands in washing anything? I found it quite interesting indeed. Mom was a reader, so after we watched the news on television and it was switched off, she gave me copies of old and recent <u>Readers' Digest</u> magazines for my reading pleasure. She also gave me some <u>National Geographic</u> magazines, whose color pictures I found to be highly interesting.

After I had been at the Salts, acclimatizing and getting used to American life, a news write-up about me and my new family appeared in the July 30, 1971 paper. My family wore my Joromi shirts and I wore my kente. The write-up said, "Stephen Kwame of Kumasi, Ghana, arrived in New York on July 19 and is now at the Walter Salts, his home during the coming year in which he'll be Jefferson High School's American Field Service student. It took 'Kwamina' ten hours by plane to New York and 30 hours during the trip by bus which took him to Minnetonka where he was met by the Salt family.

'Kwamina' (his name meaning 'a little boy born on Saturday'), is a charming representative of his country. He speaks English fluently and is looking forward to learning more about the customs of this country. His gifts to his American family included Joromi shirts for Mr. Salt and Tom. Mrs. Salt is wearing the 'Kon mu adze' which is worn by Ghanaian women. In describing it, Kwame stated the words meant 'something around the neck.' Kwamina is pictured wearing the traditional dress of his country, the 'kente' worn primarily for special occasions. It is with pleasure that Alexandrians welcome Kwamina to this vicinity."

It surely gave me a pleasant feeling that for the first time in my life, good circumstances had brought my picture and write-up in a newspaper, and an American newspaper for that matter. My white smile in the picture summed up all my elation and happiness for this accomplishment. It was the start of a series of write-ups about me in the <u>Alexandrian Press</u>.

I couldn't wait to be at school. Jefferson Senior High was going to be my academic cocoon for the year. Tom, at only sixteen, had his own car, so he took me for several visits before the regular academic year started. It was a big, red brick building which, as Tom said, was the academic habitat for more than a thousand students. It had tennis courts, a big parking lot, and a dirt track field. The grass in front of the school was a green riot and well mowed.

When we took a tour inside, the school had its own gymnasium, cafeteria, water fountains, and clean bathrooms for both boys and girls. There were some table-tennis tables close to the gym. On the wall facing the gym were several photographs of former A.F.S. students. It then occurred to me that I was only the second African who had come to Alexandria. The first was a boy from Ethiopia.

In August, almost a month after my arrival at Alexandria, Mom and Dad Salt took a fishing trip vacation to the Boundary Waters Canoe Area in the Superior National Forest, and I was lucky to be taken. Mr. Salt had a very big vehicle. It was like a house on wheels. Actually, it was a mobile home. I had never seen a vehicle which had beds, a fridge, a toilet, a kitchen, and air conditioning, all in one. Being in a mobile home was a really fantastic and exciting experience.

On August 20, Mr. Salt fixed his nice boat to the mobile home and off we were on our way to the Minnesota-Canadian border for our relaxing fishing trip.

"Have you fished before, Kwame?" Mom asked.

"No, never before."

"Well, you're going to have fun doing it soon," Mr. Salt said.

Tom chose to stay behind because he had a party to go to. Mr. Salt drove off while I was comfortably in bed and being cooled by the air conditioner. He drove long hours as we passed through Long Praire, Little Falls, and Brainerd. We continued for some time and stopped at Aitkin to visit some friends of Mom and Dad Salts'. After about an hour of relaxation from driving, where Mom Salt seemed to be proud of hosting a foreign student (she boasted to friends), we took off again and went straight north to Grand Rapids and eastward to Hibbing and on to Virginia. I remember the last town to be Tower as we approached Lake Vermilion. There were sky-blue lakes galore. I liked the verdant coloration immediately. The wilderness provided a glimpse of Minnesota in its very early days as told by teacher Mom Salt.

"Look at all the blue lakes," Mom said.

"Yes, they are beautiful and absolutely breathtaking."

"That is where we get the name Minnesota."

"Minnesota doesn't sound like an English name."

"Yes, it's true. Actually, it's an Indian name. It came from the Sioux Indians and Minnesota to them meant 'cloudy waters,' so the English translated it to 'sky-tinged waters,'" Mom sounded extra-intelligent with all this explanation. "We now refer to Minnesota as the 'land of sky-blue waters,'" Mom continued to impress.

The place was a big wilderness of azure coloration of abundant water masses and sky, and natural verdancy. The naturalness of the area was rather piquant.

We went past Lake Vermilion and camped close to Trout Lake. We were all wearied by the long travel, so we set camp by Trout Lake and unpacked. Mom cooked dinner, and after we savoured the taste of her cooking, the sun went down at about 9:30 P.M. A silky black darkness engulfed us and we pulled out our beds and slept a sound sleep.

At early dawn, we prepared our fishing gear. I had a fishing pole. We got our minnows and night crawlers and packed lunches. Dad unhitched the boat and we rowed on the lake to a good fishing spot. Dad, a natural fisherman, had a clear knowledge of where the fish were biting and we anchored. In no time, he had a bite. As if by an electrical impulse, he yanked his pole and wound up the line. In a flash, a weighty fish with bulbous glassy eyes was brought into the boat with the net by Dad.

"Wow!" shouted Mom to congratulate Dad.

"Kwame, this fish is called a walleye because of its prominent eyes," Dad said.

"In the night, if light shines on them, they brighten up," Mom said.

I was getting a lesson in fishing and wanted eagerly to have a bite myself.

"Yank it up quickly, immediately when you feel something taking your bait," Dad said, and continued, "If you see your bopper jerk suddenly, then wind up the line."

I thought I felt something take my minnow so I immediately started to wind up my line. With eagerness and anxiety, I brought up my hook only to find weeds. I was disappointed, but Dad said, "Kwame, let's go again."

He gave me a night crawler and I thought the big worm was distasteful to look at. But I hooked it anyway, and threw my hook ahead of me. Dad had landed another big one and this time it was a northern pike. After five minutes, I had a bite. With all excitement, I wound up my line and, yes, up came a good sized fish.

"Its a walleye, Dad," I said.

"Way to go, Kwame," Dad said.

"Yes, it's a big walleye!" Mom shouted. I was filled with elation and enjoying my first fishing trip already. That day I caught six beautiful walleyes and a northern-pike.

It was getting late and Dad took up the anchor, as he said we could individually take a specific number of fish. I was surprised because here was plenty of fish and I didn't see why we could only take just a small number.

"It's the law, Kwame," Dad said.

"Why?"

"If they don't protect the fish, people will overfish and deplete the fish stock."

"You see, that way other people too can have the privilege to catch fish as we caught today, Kwame, " Mom said.

"I'm beginning to understand what you mean. They protect the fish for the people's own interest."

We got to our mobile home and Mom started cleaning the fish. I thought it was a tedious job, but Mom didn't seem to mind. She cleaned, filleted the fish, and cut the heads and threw them away.

"Why are throwing the fish heads away?" I asked. "It's the best part of the fish. We eat fish heads at home in Ghana."

"There are plenty of fillets. Why should you eat the head?" Mom asked.

"There is a lot of calcium in the bony head. I have strong teeth. I can chew them."

"No, Kwame. We have plenty of fish here. Forget about the bones."

I shut my mouth, but I was surprised because I thought Americans were wasteful.

After cleaning the fish, Mom cooked up an exciting cuisine of fried walleye fillets and wild rice with some delicious sauce. The taste was exquisite, and it was the highlight of the whole trip. We had it three different times. Dad froze the rest of the fish and we relaxed with short walks around the area. There was a big elm tree just by our camp, and a week after our stay, there was the report that a bear was in the tree. I was so scared, but Dad wanted us to go and see the stray animal.

"Kwame, have you seen a bear before?"

"No."

"You want to see one?" he asked.

"No, thanks."

"Come on, don't be chicken. Let's go see it," Mom said.

"You twisted my arm. I'll go with you, but I'll stand a good distance away and watch."

As we got to the elm tree, a small group of people had already gathered close to it. The bear, a big black bear, was eating some twigs nonchalantly. It seemed not to be bothered by the watchful eyes of the humans. But the people wanted to get it out of the area and away into the surrounding forest. In a very short time, someone fired a shot into the air, and the frightened bear got down quickly and ran sideways and forwards into the dark beyond.

"Are we going to be bothered by these big wild animals?"

"Kwame, if you don't bother them, they will also leave you alone. They are just attracted by the garbage around."

The next day, Dad took us in the mobile home to a garbage dump and there we saw a gregarious group of bears, both black and brown, feeding on the dump. I was slowly getting away from my fear of bears. It was my first time of seeing so many bears together. It was a souvenir sight for keeps.

After our tenth day of fishing, we had had enough fish and relaxation. We packed our fishing gear, hitched the boat to our mobile home and said goodbye to Superior National Forest and Trout Lake. As we headed back, the trip seemed shorter. Mom continued to tell me more about Minnesota. She talked about the very fertile soil and iron ore. In fact, I knew much about the iron ore, taconite, and the Mesabi Iron Range in form three in our geography classes as St. Augustine's in Ghana. I also knew about the Great Lakes.

"Have you heard about Lake Superior?" Mom asked.

"Yes, I have. I studied it in school."

"I bet you don't know that the Chippewa Indians called it 'Kitchi Gamma.'"

"What does that mean?" I asked.

"It means 'Great Water,'" Mom said.

"Mom, you are intelligent because you know English, Sioux, and Chippewa."

"Thank you, Kwame. I just learned it in school, and, you know, I said I was a teacher."

"You were a good teacher because you know a lot."

"Thanks again, Kwame. I just did the best I could." We stopped at certain rest stops along the highway and, finally, after several hours, we were back in Alexandria again. Tom welcomed and helped us move back in.

"How was your trip, Kwame?"

"Fantastic."

"Did you catch any fish?"

"Of course I did. I caught several and you'll be eating them soon. Did you have fun yourself?"

"Yes, I did. It was a good vacation."

"What did you do and what did you have to drink?" Mom asked.

"We had punch," Tom said.

However, later, Tom told me that they were tempted to have beer but they didn,t. I told him that beer drinking and alcohol was not a big deal in

90

Africa, as anyone of any age could buy alcohol. I told him that because of the liberalization in alcohol purchase, kids don't even bother buying it. It's not a problem with us at all.

"I wish I was in your country, because here they don't allow us to drink 'til you are eighteen."

When we finished unpacking, Mom, as tired as she was, still had to cook dinner. I felt sorry for her, but she didn't seem to mind to do her duties as a wife and mother. As a matter of fact, she was all sing-song and happy about it. We watched a little bit of TV and I retired to bed. That was my first month in this strange country, with strange people who are already friends; and I saw I fitted in somehow in American life.

Chapter X

School at Jefferson Senior High School 1971-1972

School and interaction with the Jefferson High School students was the focal point of my being in America. As a foreign student, I had to give speeches to the students and staff. I was very scared because I had never given a speech anywhere before. I was a bit lucky, though, because back at St. Augustine's in Ghana, when I was a class prefect, I had to give announcements and small talk in front of my classmates but really that was about it in speech giving. That was even very informal. I was very anxious indeed.

A week before school started, I went to Jefferson to register my classes Miss Ludwig (may she rest in peace) helped me. I registered for chemistry, biology (audit class), American literature, French, social studies, and history. She said American history was mandatory, so I had no arguments with her. It was all anxiety to go to high school in America.

Tom drove me in his Chevrolet to school the first day, and I was met by the A.F.S. president of the school, Barry Arvold. He was a blondish, handsome-looking guy who was a junior. With a smile (I always remember his smile), he and Tom took me to the principal's office. The principal was Mr. Wayne Elton. A handsome smile greeted me. Mr. Elton welcomed me to the school and announced and introduced me to the students on the school's intercom. Of course, I was the only black there, so no one could miss me. Everybody was trying to be nice and said hi. I kept losing my way to my classrooms and had to ask directions from other students. They all gladly responded to my needs. The American classrooms were much unlike Ghana. Whereas in Ghana there used to be at least forty people in a classroom, the population in Jefferson classrooms was much smaller. In Ghana too, the students stayed in their classrooms and it was the duty of the teachers to come to class. In the United States, though, the teachers stayed in their classrooms and the students went to the teachers' classrooms. There were always about three-minute breaks between classes to allow the students to get to their different classrooms after each period.

In Ghana, too, we used to have eight forty-minute classes a day. There were two recesses, one at nine o'clock and the other, a ten-minute break, at noon. Classes closed at ten after two in the afternoon.

My first class in the United States was Mr. Krump's chemistry. I remember Mr. Krump gave us homework the very first day. Mr. Reuter's literature class was boring and Mr. Wittenberg's history class was interesting. It also had a good number of students. I liked Mr. Pohl's French class because I thought it was very easy.

At lunch, I went to the cafeteria and had lunch with Roger Heegaard and Paul Trumm. Roger was the son of a doctor and Paul's father was a pharmacist. Roger was about my height, 5'8", was handsome and had a handsome pair of legs … he was wearing shorts. He also had natural curly hair. Roger was going to be a wonderful friend all year. Well liked by most of the girls at Jefferson, Roger was a popular student, so I was glad to be a friend of his.

I enjoyed my first day at school very much. When school closed in the afternoon, Tom was waiting for me in his car and he drove me home.

"Hi, welcome back. How was school?" Mrs. Salt asked both of us as she offered us some cookies and milk.

"I liked it, thanks," I said.

"Kwame was introduced to the whole school by Mr. Elton, our principal."

"I got a kick out of that. All the students in my chemistry class turned to look at me and say hi."

"Well, did you get any homework?"

"Yes, I did. I have some in chemistry and French."

"I can't help you then because I never took chemistry or French," Mom Salt said.

"I am free for today, but I've got to practice my bassoon, " Tom said.

"Oh, you play an instrument, eh?"

"Yes, I do. Did you ever take music?"

"Yes, I took music theory and had a chance to play the piano at St. Augustine's, but I never had the fees and time."

"You should have learned how to play," Tom said. "Here at Jefferson we are very musically inclined," he continued.

As we finished eating our chocolate chip cookies, I went to the basement and changed. Tom came down and played Led Zeppelin, Santana, and Credence Clearwater Revival songs on his nice stereo. He was giving me an initiation into rock and roll, and I remember I liked Led Zeppelin a lot. Back home in Ghana, the students were in love with the music of James Brown, (especially "Papa's got a brand new bag," "Say it loud, I am black and proud," etc.), Otis Redding, Wilson Picket, and Aretha Franklin. I loved music of all kinds from classical music, soul, The Beatles' music, and right now, rock and roll.

After listening for a while, Tom asked, "How would you like to go for a ride in our pontoon?"

"I would love that."

We went outside to the dock on Lake Darling in front of our house and got into the vehicle. Tom let us put our safety jackets on and turned the motor on also as we rowed slowly away from the dock and into the clear open waters of Lake Darling. There were some fishermen on the lake. Some people were water-skiing in three-speed boats ahead of us. Tom rode the pontoon towards Arrowwood Lodge across the lake from our house. The wind was down and the sky blue. Occasionally, I would hear the loud piercing cry of a loon. I could see fish swimming in the clear lake. As we almost reached Arrowwood, Tom turned left and we headed for the creek. We rowed slowly and comfortably. Everybody was white, and on seeing a black person, they waved. The whole cruise was pleasant and relaxing. When we got back to the house, Mrs. Salt was cooking.

"How would you like steak and baked potatoes for supper?" I discovered later that Americans loved steak a lot.

"I would love it," I said, although I didn't have the slightest idea of what steak was.

"Kwame, did you ever have apple pie?" Mom Salt asked.

"No, we used to have meat pies in Ghana, but not apple pie."

"Well, you haven't been to America if you haven't eaten apple pie," Tom said.

"In America it's hamburgers, hot dogs, and apple pie. These are typical American foods," Mrs. Salt said.

I was really looking forward to trying all these novelties, so I couldn't wait for supper. Tom and I helped set the table. Tom taught me how to set the table with the knife, fork, spoon, and the napkin. He allowed me to pour the milk. At about six o'clock, food was ready, and Dad Salt joined us from his room. He never talked much. The meal was very delectable indeed. I savored and relished the taste of steak, baked potatoes steaming with butter and, most of all, the apple pie with vanilla ice cream. Mrs. Salt was a good cook. When supper was over, we rinsed the plates, glasses, and the cutlery and put them in the dishwasher.

The day had been good. I did my homework and watched selected programs on TV. Mrs. Salt let me watch Flip Wilson because she, herself, liked Flip. Back in Ghana, my father was the only one in the whole neighborhood with a fourteen-inch black and white Sanyo television, so I knew about certain American programs. I asked Mrs. Salt, "Do you sometimes see 'Bonanza,' 'The Invisible Man,' and 'Lassie'?"

"Yes, we have them all here, but they are really old programs," she said.

"I liked all the good people, especially the Cartwright family, in 'Bonanza.' Did you, Tom?"

"Yes, Kwame. I thought they were good people and good horse riders, too."

"That's for sure," Mrs. Salt said.

At about 8:30, Mrs. Salt switched the TV off. Tom practiced his bassoon, and I read more old copies of <u>Readers' Digest</u> and looked, once again, at the pictures in the <u>National Geographic</u> magazines.

Tom continued to practice Handel's music on his instrument. I could tell he was a good player because I had heard some of Handel's music in Ghana, and I knew how they went. Tom was not making many mistakes.

Mr. Salt had all the time been in his rocking chair and never talked. At ten o'clock Mrs. Salt asked us to go to bed, and we obeyed immediately. In bed I prayed to thank God for bringing me to America and into this family. I was already attached to Mrs. Salt, for she seemed to know a lot and was always seeking what would make me happy.

The following morning, I got up very early, took a shower, brushed my teeth, and went upstairs. Mrs. Salt was already up and cooking some oatmeal and frying some eggs and bacon for our breakfast.

"How would you like to set the table, Kwame?"

"Sure."

I was always happy to help around the house, so I got everything on the table and poured milk also. Tom came up without brushing his teeth and ate his breakfast before going back to get his teeth cleaned. I was so surprised at this because I could never eat while my teeth were never brushed because of the funny taste in my mouth and morning breath. Tom, however, didn't seem to mind. We set off to school once again in his Chevrolet. That was our routine for the rest of the first semester.

At school too, there were many extracurricular activities apart from the academics. I was on the school representative council and I joined the cross-country team. On the team, I met friends like Gary Lusso, Wally Drexler, Bob Reuter, and Francis Lukes. I found cross-crountry training and meets to be very, very, very tedious and tiring, but I always braved the elements to run five miles every weekend. Our cross-country coach, Mr. Bun Fisher, was a religious man, and rather old with white hair who instilled strong discipline both morally and at training and meets. We always prayed before running. I remember our first meet was at Glenwood and we ran on a hilly golf course. I was so wearied that I came in tenth. I liked the sport just because it gave us (the athletes) the opportunity to travel within Minnesota. I remember we ran in Glenwood, Benson, Albert Lea, Bemidji, Brainerd, Breckenridge, Detroit Lakes, Fergus Falls, Little Falls, Long Prairie, etc.

I wasn't very successful at cross-country; however, the training was giving me a head start for track and field the following semester. It was at one of such cross-country meets that I met a nice, voluptuous girl from Argentina. Her name was Maria Eugenia Gallo, and the Americans called her Geny for short. Geny spoke English very well, although her native language was Spanish. She was the A.F.S. student at Elbow Lake from Argentina. I thought Geny was very good looking with dark curly hair and soft dark eyes. She was impressed to meet me and gave me her address and telephone number. It was the start of a very beautiful friendship that was to last through the 1971-1972 academic year and beyond.

It was already cold in Minnesota, but snow had not fallen yet. I was quite anxious to see my first snow and surely it came with a bang. I was with

Tom when it started to snow. In my ignorance, I asked Tom, "Where are all these tiny, white bugs coming from?"

Tom laughed and said, "Kwame, that's snow falling."

Sure enough, it was, because the snow melted to touch. However, it continued to snow and the ground and everywhere was covered with a carpet of snow. Everywhere was white. It was a serene whiteness which epitomized God's own soul, I thought. I liked snow and made some snowballs. They felt cold to touch. I played in the snow everyday until cross-country was over.

I remember very clearly Homecoming 1971. I attended the occasion with my date, and you guessed it: my date was Geny. I had written to Geny to be my date, and she promptly accepted. The occasion was fun galore and a collage of excitement and emotion.

The festivities got underway when Cozy Olson was elected and crowned the new queen. There were five pretty girls with their escorts. There was also a raucous pep fest; we had a wet but exciting parade and a parking lot bonfire and a thrilling football contest. There was a happy dance and a generous helping of excitement and spirit. That was Homecoming of 1971.

I was part of the festivities, for I was paraded and chauffeured in a convertible by Tom Conn. I wore my native dress for special occasions- the kente. The royal court included Carla Solum and Dawn Norlien. Rick Banke, Roger Heegaard, and Bruce Smith were all senior escorts. Dan Gaugert sang the theme song of "You've Got a Friend."

Following the crowning ceremonies, attention was shifted downtown for the parade. While the excited Jefferson High School Cardinal Band led the way with several lively numbers, the procession quickly found its way back to Jefferson and to the bonfire. Although it was raining, most students still had enough loudness in them to give enthusiasm at the Friday Pep Fest and shout their encouragements to the team as they took on students from the town of Sinclair-Lewis- Sauk Centre - in the evening's football contest. Even though Alex lost, a great second half come back by the team and a fine half-time marching performance by the band provided the fans with a great show. And, as I danced with beautiful Geny in her flowery dress at the Saturday dance, Homecoming 1971 took its place among the fond memories of Kwame and other Jeffersonians.

I had never been kissed by any girl in my life, and I wished greatly that Geny would kiss me, but she didn't. Like myself, she was a strict Catholic and in this church, any show of romance before marriage was considered a sin. I was very disappointed, but I took it in stride.

On Sunday morning, we were driven to St. Mary's Catholic Church for Mass. Geny and I both received communion and we were happy for the body of Chirist. Since there was school on Monday, Rob drove Geny back to Elbow Lake. Of course, I went along with them, and had a good time with Geny's family, the Fjosliens. I had, over the weekend, enjoyed one of the most popular high school festivities in America. It was a good time.

Chapter XI

My First Halloween, Thanksgiving and Christmas in America. 1971

The first semester was almost coming to an end. I had been involved in many activities, and given speeches here and there, and danced the Ewe <u>agbadja</u> to the utter enjoyment and amazement of my audiences. I used to sing Ashanti and Fanti songs to delight my audiences and showed them postcards from Ghana and some interesting places in Kumasi. I taught them how to count to ten in my indigenous African language, and I explained that among the Ashantis and Fantis, every person knew the exact day of the week he was born because our first names were dedicated to these days. I told them that:

"Kwesi" meant a boy born on Sunday, and "Esi" was a girl born on Sunday.

"Kojo" was a boy born on Monday. "Adwoa" was a girl born on Monday.

"Kobina" was a Tuesday boy; "Abena" was a Tuesday girl.

"Kwaku" was a Wednesday boy; "Akua" was a Wednesday girl.

"Yaw" was a Thursday boy; "Yaa" was a Thursday girl.

"Kofi" was a Friday boy; "Afua" was a Firday girl.

And finally, "Kwame," my name, meant a boy born on Saturday, and "Ama," a girl born on Saturday.

After explaining all these, there was always the curious question:

"What if there were many children in the same family born on the same day?" I've heard Africans like large families." I would then explain that apart from these names we also had many local second names. I told them that in my family alone there were three Kwames. My father is called Kwame Bosomafi; I am called Kwame Mbroh; and my brother, after me, was called Kwame Skete. I also explained that apart from these nice names, the missionaries asked us to take Christian names when we were baptized. They said you're then protected by a patron saint. Thus, I got "Stephen" to be my Christian name. The priest who baptized me said St. Stephen was the first martyr for believing in Jesus Christ and was stoned to death for his faith, so I should strongly believe in God and Jesus, take Him as my personal savior and obey, worship, and revere Him always. I never forgot the priest's words. I tell my audiences that I've always done just that. Alleluia! My audiences usually clapped at this. Amen!

It was very cold and already nearing zero and below zero weather on the thermometer. One thing interesting about homes in Minnesota is that every home had a thermometer inside the house and another outside it. They, therefore, never missed the temperature in winter. In Ghana, we could care less about temperature because it was always the same, eighty-five degrees, except, of course, during the dry Harmattan season when we felt the weather was too hot, maybe in the nineties or even a hundred. It was so cold that people thought it was awfully warm when the thermometer read ten below zero, because for some time it was constantly registering twenty below zero with the wind chill. I felt like a black Eskimo. For me, an African brought to Minnesota for the first time, extreme cold weather was hard to take, but I braved it to run every weekend, go out and make snowballs, build a snowman, try ice skating, and become an avid ice hockey and broomball spectator and player.

Students like Pam and Patsy Ziegelman taught me sliding on ice, and also tobogganing and snowmobiling. There were always many sports and games to be played in winter to help alleviate constant thoughts about the monstrous cold.

After celebrating Halloween, and Thanksgiving with the usual traditional turkey and dressing, the town of Alexandria took an altogether different aspect. Downtown Alexandria was decorated with green pine trees, flashing red, white, and blue lights and also red ribbons, to await Christmas. I was very anxious to see an American Christmas for the first time.

At this time, there were shoppers galore. All the shops were filled to the brim with shoppers. I learned in America, it was customary to give a gift at Christmas. Everywhere I went in shops, restaurants, and theatres, the atmosphere was permeated with ubiquitous Christmas carols and songs. I heard Bing Crosby's "White Christmas" for the first time and liked it. I remembered the songs I learned in Ghana about winter. I remembered:

> "In the bleak midwinter
> Long, long ago
> Snow had fallen
> Snow on snow
> Snow on snow
> In the bleak midwinter
> Long, long ago."

Many times, I would hear "Handel's Messiah" and the "Hallelujah Chorus." There was no place that Christmas was celebrated with such intensity and electrical vigor than in the United States of America. Alexandria and Minnesota were doing too well portraying Christmas to me.

A couple of weeks before Christmas, I remember I got a start when the Homecoming queen herself, Cozy Olson, asked me for a date. Cozy was strikingly beautiful. She was tall and had long dark hair. Her smile was radiant, for she had perfect teeth as white as snow. Her name and demeanor suggested comfort and warmth. "Is this really me?" I had a strong feeling of "fait accompli" and a strong sense of high self-esteem as I reminisce on this, for Cozy, as beautiful as she was, as a most wonderful date.

She apologized profusely when she was five minutes late. Actually, she was caught waiting at the railway intersection as a cargo train was crossing the road. And you know American trains. They are too long and have too many coaches.

I put on the best clothes I had, and put on cologne too. The delay had made me very nervous, for it was my first date ever with an American girl, and it had to be with the Homecoming queen. I kept looking at my watch after every five seconds. Finally, I looked out at the window and saw a yellow Volkswagen. It was Cozy. She rang the doorbell and my heart sank a spondaic beat. Mrs. Salt opened the door and in she came and filled the room with exuberance and radiance. With a perfect smile, she said, "Hi, is Kwame ready?"

"Hi, come on in," Mrs. Salt said.

"Hi, Kwame. Sorry I am late. I had to wait at the railway intersection because of a train. I hope you didn't think I had disappointed you."

"It's alright, Cozy. I knew you would never fail me. Thanks."

"Can we go now?" she asked.

"Sure, I'm ready."

"Have fun, you guys," Mrs. Salt said.

"Thank you," both Cozy and myself said simultaneously.

Cozy apologized again and I told her she shouldn't bother very much. I told her about African time and African punctuality, and Cozy was relieved that I didn't mind waiting. In a very suave manner, she held me in conversation. Now, come to think of it, her erudition was quite poignant, even at that age. I enjoyed every bit of it.

When we got to the place of our date, there were the most popular boys and girls of Jefferson. Roger Heegaard was there. So was John Bale, Paul Trumm, Dan Gaugert, and Gary Bakken. Pam and Patsy Ziegelman were there too. Barb de Grote, Margaret Benesh, and Jodi Wentz were there. Joe Perino and Riley McCarten were also there. I felt elated with all these beautiful and intelligent students, the cream of the crop of Jefferson Senior High School. I was very proud of myself indeed. It was a Beta party so we played games, sat around, and talked and plain had fun. We had pop and punch refreshments. We had not been keeping track of time and when she brought me home, it was a bit past the time Mrs. Salt gave us. Cozy actually kissed me! Whooeii! Was this really me? Did she like me this much? What thing about me made her like me this much? That night, I sat long hours pondering on these questions. Before I knew it, I was in contented slumber land (and dreaming a handful about Cozy). She became a truly good friend all year and she wrote this in my yearbook. I still have it.

"Kwame, I am so glad I dared ask you to that Beta thing, 'cuz, otherwise, I would probably never have gotten to know you. Thanks so much for going with me. It was so fun, but I'm sorry about getting you home so late. You're really a neat person. I'm proud to be a friend of yours. If you ever come back to Alexandria, be sure and try to see me. I hope your life is full of happiness. Thanks for being <u>you</u>. Cozy."

After the year, I never saw Cozy again, even though I kept coming back to visit Alexandria during my college and graduate school days and even at our just ended twentieth year class reunion which I attended all the way from Africa. Dear reader, you'll also hear about this but be patient.

It was during the winter of 1971 that I met my real white father. He was Mr. Aga, a very humane, magnanimous, charitable, and pleasant man who, at that time, owned KXRA, the radio station in Alexandria. He was also a newspaper columnist. When I look back on the great things, letters, and money this man has given me, then he, surely, deserves a place in heaven, for there is no one as kind and altruistic as my father. He still cares a tremendous lot about me.

Things were not all that honky-dory between Tom and myself although Tom, Mrs. Salt and Walter loved me a great deal. It was very sad when I switched host parents to come and live with Rob and our father and mother, Mr. Aga and his wife Nora, just before Christmas for the remainder of my A.F.S. school year. I will never regret that change because of this great man, Mr. Aga. In fact, this whole book, if it ever sees publication, is dedicated to Mr. Aga for his downright magnanimity and warmth.

What I remember most about my father is his voice- a steady sweet metallic and sonorous bass -a radio voice which could send joyous chills of warmth to everyone he touched. He really did touch many lives and continues to do so. I just talked to him on the phone.

He goes, "Hello."

"This is Kwame," I say.

"Oh, Kwame, I'll be darned. We just got here from town. How is my boy?"

"I am fine."

"Yup, what a boy you are, Kwame. Do you have a job yet?"

"I have a temporary job which pays minimum wage, $4.25 an hour."

"Well, you've got to start somewhere, Kwame."

"I guess so."

"Well, Kwame, these telephone calls don't cost that much if you make them short. Always keep in touch and write us one of those wonderful letters of yours. Keep hanging in there, and God bless you."

"Thanks, Dad. Bye for now." I hung up and it was such a relief to hear that voice again.

Now let's go back to my first Christmas with my new family with whom I had just come to live. There was a pervasive Christmas aura in the house. The huge, decorated Christmas pine tree stood to the right of the furnace. The fire crackled in it, although the house had central heating. Dad kept poking it. The tree flickered its multicolored lights. The cold wind howled outside.

"Yup, Kwame, have a seat."

"Thank you."

"Now, Kwame, we are very glad to have you. Always feel at home here. I betch ya, Kwame, you never saw a Christmas as cold and white as this one, did ya?"

"No, never, but it is a good and welcome change."

"You'll have fun. You really will have fun, Kwame. What a great boy you are."

"Thanks again."

"What would you like for Christmas?"

"Anything, Dad. It doesn't take much to make me happy. In fact, I am happy already being here as part of your family."

"Yup, Kwame. We are too. We-e re-all-y are," he said the last sentence as if singing. "How would you like to go to town with us for shopping?"

"I sure would."

"Erc, where are we going?" Nora, my mom, who always called her husband by the first name, interrupted.

"As soon as you're done in the kitchen, Sweetheart," Dad always called mom "Norie" or "Sweetheart."

The Aga family was a sixsome: Mom, Dad, Dick, Marilyn, Kathryn, and Rob. Dick, the oldest was married to Fran, and they have a son called Scottie. Marilyn was married to John Roesler and their newborn baby boy, Michael, was with them. Kathryn was married to George, a tall, thin fellow. Rob was a junior and Kwame, myself, was a senior, the A.F.S. foreign student from Ghana, and a track star at Jefferson. All my white brothers and sisters had arrived at our house for Christmas and the whole place was pulsating with a happy family togetherness and Christmas joy.

When Mom was done in the kitchen, Dad, Mom, Rob and myself hopped in Dad's luxurious blue Buick and we were off to the shopping centers in downtown Alexandria. There was frantic shopping. The shops were jam packed. Even at that young age, I thought these people were side-tracking the meaning of Christmas:

"Joy to the world!
the Lord is come;
Let Earth receive her king;
Let every heart prepare Him room
And heaven and nature sing
And heaven and nature sing
And heaven and nature sing."

and just inundating themselves with materialism. Or maybe it's not just America. It's the whole Christendom. Alas! Christ, our Savior, is born … be happy. That's the message.

When we went to Herbergers, Mom bought me some nice flower-patterned warm quilts and an electric blanket.

"These sure will keep you warm," she said.

"Thank you very much."

Dad bought me a warm woolen coat, a Viking stocking cap, some thermal socks, and two pairs of warm leather gloves. We went to the shoe store, and Mom and Rob selected a pair of warm boots for me. I was very grateful indeed. My gratitude was only manifested by an ear-to-ear smile and an honest, sincere warm and appreciative "Thank you, Dad, thank you, Mom, and thank you, Rob," a definite sincere African show of gratefulness.

"Oh, Kwame, you are welcome," Mom said.

We went to Sears, the shopping mall, and other places for more shopping. I got a kick out of the painstaking way the salespeople wrapped the boxes with colorful Christmas wrapping paper and ribbons. Surely, America is a different world, very much unlike a third world country like Ghana in Africa because, back home, you definitely won't get that service.

As I immersed myself in the beautiful Christmas atmosphere in the United States, I kept thinking about home and my family in Ghana. I kept asking myself, "Will my father be able to afford the traditional chicken for the whole eleven of them?" I now saw how very blessed I had been by being in America. When we finished shopping, the car's booth was filled with

Christmas packages. These packages formed a colorful mountain under the huge light-flickering Christmas tree.

On Christmas Eve, after a sumptuous dinner, we relaxed with convivial conversation and at about nine o'clock, we were gathered around the tree where Dad took a package, one at a time, and read the card bearing who it was for. Many presents exchanged hands and to say that I was happy is a big understatement, because even though I had been in this home only a little while back, I still got as many presents as the head of the house himself. This Christmas show of lofty generosity, to me, surely epitomized the very welcome American hospitality in a poignant fashion. Is this what America is? Is it all giving and not taking? Will these showers of magnanimity continue? Hopefully yes! And so they did all year and even beyond. They still trickle down to today. The psalmist said, "When I look at the wilderness, I ask, 'Where does my help come from? My help comes from the Lord!'"

The good Lord was helping me by introducing me to good people and He worked miracles through them to bestow strength to a weak and wearied spirit like mine. Mr. Aga provided succor to my most fatigued spirit. And it was he who God chose to be a helper to Kwame. The Ashantis and Fantis have a proverb that goes, "When God creates a poor person, He also creates the poor person's helper." As poor as I was, I found my helper. I found my other daddy in Mr. Aga of Alexandria, Minnesota.

At his house, things began to take shape for me in America. The Christmas season and festivities ended abruptly after New Year's Day. When 1972 was ushered in at a New Year's Eve New York vigil, I blessed my soul and said, "Kwame, you are a real achiever and blessed for you are truly in God's country."

There's no gain-saying that America is truly God's country indeed. At that time, God's country was under the leadership of President Nixon, and the Vietnam War was still raging and claiming many American soldiers' lives.

After Christmas, I still continued to run in preparation for track and field the upcoming semester. Every morning, in spite of the biting cold, I would wear thermal underwear and a workout suit I had gotten from Mr. Bun Fisher, our coach, and run towards Arrowwood Lodge. It was icy on the road and the hard ice made me develop shin splints which ached so terribly. I was really looking forward to track.

When school reopened, Bun Fisher, a typical Americal coach, believed in hard work and knew, sincerely, that it was only through vigorous training that would lift us to higher heights. His attitude reminded me of St. Augustine's College school motto, "Omnia Vincit Labor," that is, "Labor Conquers All." Our motto of hard work, combined with Bun Fisher's solid trust in God and the black althlete, made him assign me to the 440 yards- a long sprint race -one of the most difficult races on the track. My job was to sprint once around a standard track field. Today, in metric terms, it is the 400 meters. He also let me try the 100 yards and the 220 yards, but soon I discovered that I couldn't beat Jack Geris in both shorter sprints so my real area of concentration was the 440.

At our first meet in Glenwood, I was first in the 440 and second in both the 100 and 220 yards.

"Am I then an athlete?" I couldn't help asking myself. I trained harder and soon, I was gaining fame in my district. I set meet records at Little Falls. I lettered in varsity track and was proud to be presented with the coveted red and black leather jacket of Jefferson Senior High School. I was a real jock. I was steadily gaining fame in my area. The highlight of my running career was during the Regional Track Meet which took place at Glenwood. At that time, my girlfriend, Geny Gallo, had been invited to watch me run, so I really had to run hard to impress her. According to pre-meet times, I was an underdog because Moorhead and Brainerd really had fantastic runners. Of course, everywhere I went in Minnesota, I was the only black guy there and you know everybody knew the athletic prowess of the strong black man in America. Coming from Africa was no different.

We were called to our marks after stretching out. I was in lane two and the favorite, the guy from Brainerd, was in lane one. Somebody from Little Falls had a false start. After a brief period of gamboling, we were called to our marks again. At the sound of the gun, still the nervous Little Falls guy jumped the gun again so he was disqualified. We gamboled still further and came back to our marks. This time everything was honky-dory and I took off, out of my blocks, in a doubly fast acceleration. I had had a very good start. I increased in acceleration with all my strength and running power and was way ahead by the 200 yard bend. I maintained my top speed until the 300 yard mark, where I began to feel fatigue in my muscles. I didn't relent and pushed and forged ahead. I never looked behind me. All the spectators were on their feet and Jefferson High School students yelled on top of their voices. I just had to win. When I hit the tape, I was so tired that I stumbled and fell, but I had won the gold medal and that was all that mattered.

The next day, my picture was in the <u>Echo</u>, the Alexandria newspaper displaying my win and my stumbling. It was a beautiful action-packed picture which I have kept until today. The write-up went:

"KWAME MENDS won the 440 yard dash at the Region 6 track meet by diving across the finish line. Just after hitting the tape above, Kwame stumbled and fell, but he had the first place medal. Kwame really ran his heart out in the race and had his best time of the year."

After the meet, I had qualified for the (state) all-Minnesota high school track meet at Macalester College, the alma mater of Kofi Annan (the former United Nations secretary general) in St. Paul. Geny was really proud of me. She came to the field, helped me up, and held my hand. A.F.S. had brought three countries together at the meet: Ghana, Argentina, and the United States. If things were going well in the world, these countries would be the best of friends.

Everybody congratulated me, and my happiness that summarized my life's continued achievement, and a strong spirit was quite pronounced indeed. At the state track meet, Bun Fisher said it was just like the Olympics, and just the idea of participating was the main thing. I ran and lost my race in the heats as I met black guys from around the Twin cities who were better runners. In fact, the 440 yards at the state meet was won, incidentally, by a deaf guy who couldn't hear the gun but had to watch when other runners took off at the start. That is a brief synopsis of my athletic life in track in the United States.

Chapter XII

Meeting of World Teenagers for
Midwinter Ceremonies 1972

School continued with winter activities, and I remember Jefferson Senior High School's midwinter celebration. There was coronation of midwinter royalty. The royal court consisted of Princess Jodi Wentz (a real good dancer), Prince Don Snellson, Margaret Benesh, Barb de Grote, Steve Thompson, Rick Banke, and Kwame.

Many foreign exchange students from neighboring towns joined our school for the annual American Field Service (A.F.S.) assembly and stayed throughout the rest of the activities. Among the A.F.S. students were my own country girl, Mary Anne Addo, with whom I had traveled to Minnetonka from New York, and she was staying at the Floyd Boline home in Golden Valley, Minneapolis; Jackie Pivac of Auckland, New Zealand, staying at the Daniel Johnson home in Dassel; Laurits Hansen of Denmark at the David Maas home in Canby; Julie Woodward of Australia at the Don Gray home in Long Prairie; Merle Casem of the Phillippines, with the Ed Reddy's of Breckenridge. There were also Roberto Cavichioli of Brazil residing at the George Schuler home in Breckenridge; Rodney May of Australia with the Elmwood Sather family in Madison; Kenzi Karaski of Japan residing with Myron Sandbergs of Little Falls; my own girlfriend, Geny (Maria Eugenia Gallo), of Argentina residing with the Fjosliens of Elbow Lake; and Matty Llosa of Peru with the Joe Givens family of Dawson. That leaves myself, Kwame Mends, of Ghana with the Walt Salt and the Aga families of

Alexandria. I hope all these families are still alive and have fond memories of their A.F.S. sons and daughters of 1971-1972.

All the twelve foreign students representing every corner of the world were there. We appeared on KCMT TV on the "Welcome In" program before attending the basketball game and festivities which followed. We were entertained at dinner at Central School by the A.F.S. club. Following the game, a party was given in our honor at the Richard Arvold house. Our A.F.S. president, Barry Arvold, organized it.

We were also guests at the Alexandria Chamber of Commerce. As manager, Mr. Harvey Hammegren (may he rest in peace) opened the famous Runestone Museum for us. We gave speeches at the midwinter activities and I remember clearly my speech. Speaking to more than about a thousand people, I had prepared a small speech and wasn't going to embarrass myself. I used Dr. Kwegyir Aggrey's allegory of Black and White Piano Keys.

My speech went: "My principal, guardians, and parents, honorable members of staff, honorable A.F.S. foreign students, and fellow students of Jefferson, it gives me honorable pleasure to be called upon to address this gathering." People clapped for my strong beginning and courage.

When the applause died down, I continued, "I am very grateful and privileged to be in Alexandria as the only black person in a vicinity of about 100 mile radius, but I've enjoyed myself." Some in the audience laughed.

"It reminds me of the harmony we can find in one another by living together as friends. There was a certain wise educator from my country. In fact, he studied in America and married an American girl. He said, 'You can play a melody by just using white keys on the piano; you can play a good melody by just using the black keys, but for harmony, out of this world, you've got to combine and use both white and black keys. Similarly, black and white people can live together in harmony, each bringing the best out of his culture and strengthening the melting pot. Diversity of cultures makes a better country.' The United States is a great country which will continue to see abundant greatness. Thank you, A.F.S., for giving me an opportunity to live here for one year. It's a big privilege indeed and I will never, ever forget this special year as long as I live. Thank you very much."

I got wide applause and a standing ovation for this little speech. As I look back now, I had given a speech about integration and harmonious black and white togetherness but, alas, there weren't any blacks there to listen to it. Mary Anne Addo and myself were the only blacks, but, of course, we weren't from America. We were Africans. After the festivity, Geny and Mary Anne came to congratulate me. I saw Geny was very proud of me. Mary Anne invited me to come to Golden Valley for a weekend, which I did, and had a wonderful time. At that time, I should have asked Mary Anne to be my girlfriend as I could have seen her often, even when we returned to Ghana because her high school, Wesley Girls, and mine, St. Augustine's were in the same town of Cape Coast. Now, as I sit here writing and remembering her beautiful smile, I really did myself a big disservice for not asking because then I thought she really liked me. I was such a ignorant neophyte at romance that the thought never occurred to me. Maybe, also, it was our strict upbringing in a Ghanaian Catholic boys boarding high schools.

Anyway, after my speech, we were supposed to go out for snow sculptures and a girls' broomball game. However, the unbearably cold weather put a halt to these two outdoor activities. To conclude with the midwinter occasions, a very entertaining dance was held at Lincoln School on Saturday night with a live band. I danced with both Geny and Mary Anne and some Jeffersonian girls. On Valentine's Day, I sent Geny and Mary Anne Valentine cards. Geny sent a belated one back.

The winter had been long and blustery cold. I was getting tired of it, so I greatly looked forward to spring, the only season I had not seen yet in America. It was slowly warming up and snow had given way to cold showers and sometimes hail. The buds were sprouting already. The aquatic tribe of blue teal, merganser, and geese were back; the ducks zigzagged in bursts of frenzied motion, and geese flew low in a V shape flight. The ice and snow on the lakes were slowly slushy and the sound made when one stepped in slush accentuated spring. Spring also brought ideas of rebirth of the earth, for the bare trees were slowly greening and birds, squirrels chirped their contentment away. Most of these animals were on a mating spree. Farmers began a rustic life of quiet, hardworking integrity.

I was glad to put away my heavy woolen coat, stop wearing long thermal underwear, put away my stocking cap, and free my hands and fingers from almost a six-month incarceration in gloves. Spring also brought about the irremediable mealancholy of the year coming to an end for me, for, in less than three months, I would be heading home to mother Ghana and Africa.

"Will I ever come back to the United States of America again?"

That was the question I kept asking myself. However, very fortunately, I had Mr. Aga, my father, who had strong faith in my becoming a doctor in the future on account of my excellent high school grades, and promised that after I left the States, he would do everything to bring me back to go to college. He kept his promise.

As the year was fast closing, Mom and Dad took me and Rob on a vacation to Duluth, an inland port city on Lake Superior. We had a blast of a time. When we returned to Alexandria, I started getting my things together and packed. At school, my A.F.S. president, Barry Arvold, gave me a lot of records of Led Zeppelin and Santana as the A.F.S. club's appreciation for a totally satisfying cross-cultural experience.

"Let these be souvenirs from us," he said.

Pretty soon, the school yearbook was out. Mr. Knowles, the school's vice principal, a no-nonsense man whom I adored but incurred the displeasure of many recalcitrant students, gave me my yearbook with my name embossed in gold on it. Many students signed my yearbook and I would like to share some of the signatures with the reader. I guess if he doesn't know much about me by now, the signatures will tell him. Here we go:

This was a long one from Geny, the Argentinian; "Kwame, it's really hard to write something good here. My brain will get sore. My Kwame, it will be impossible to forget somebody like you because when God works as hard as He did in you, He gets really great results. Ghana someday will be proud about Kwame. And that day, a little girl from Argentina will be feeling important because one year (1971-1972), she got a tiny place in your heart. Please don't ever forget me, or at least don't forget the great moments on A.F.S. weekends- when you came to Elbow Lake, and we talked in the stairway, and we danced in the cafeteria. Afterwards, the kids would tease me about you because you were black. I didn't mind them. I thought of you as a cool guy and it surprised me to get your letter. Then I saw you in your town in my first A.F.S. weekend, and it was most fun, truly.

"After that, what we shared were letters, a lot of them, those that when you got into that business called 'track' started being far away between each other, all full of excuses and then something great, my heart trembling; you asked me to your prom!! Beautiful night. You like a diplomat, eveybody looking at us and me feeling a lot groovy. The dinner, the music played, and the game with toy guns.

"At Watertown, cool time too when I was supposed to go to that dance with you and we couldn't make it. I felt mad!! Afterwards, more letters and until now when I started feeling the pain that seeing you depart causes. Oh, man! How I got to love this groovy guy from Ghana.

"Now go home, Kwame. Go and do what God has for you. Go and make me proud of you. Go and heal people, and be president and have a family and have a little chick from Argentina in mind. Remember she loves you millions of pounds. Jesus is in you forever and you'll do cool. My gosh, we really have reasons to believe we have God. Must be great for Him to look down from up there and see that if He put us on earth, it was to love each other. I said I knew I wouldn't see you again, and I still think so. The job He has done for you will take you a lot of time. It will be hard to plan a trip to Argentina, but I still have hope. Maybe someday when I'm walking around in heaven, I'll see a big, white smile and then I'll repeat myself, 'I have God!!'- because I'll be seeing you again. Again joy will be present in my soul and you'll be saying, 'Of course, chick, I am a groovy man.' Don't quit whistling, and making people happy. And right here I stop. I've been trying to express to you how extremely HAPPY you made my year, how full of love I am. You see, it just took two sentences to finish it, something groovy, man!

"I LOVE YOU in the name of our lord Jesus. May His spirit fill your life with happiness, good moments, joy, etc. From my heart, praying for you, the best, somebody who has the honor to be considered your friend. BIG LOVE.

"P.S. Don't forget this weekend at your home either 27 and 28 of June in the Great year of God 1972. Maria Eugenia Gallo, Castelli 129, Santiago del Estera, R. Argentina. Bye till Heaven."

Until now, I never saw Geny again. However, in 1981, while I was studying for my Master's at Ohio State University, Nora, my American mom, wrote to tell me that Geny had returned to America to visit her host parents, and I should make it a point to come to Minnesota. I never made it. But I called Geny and heard her sweet compassionate voice again, and talked for about thirty minutes. That was the last time I heard from Geny.

How about this signature by Barb Freeman, a junior who sat in front of me in trigonometry class. Our teacher was Mr. Schwartz.

"Kwame, I guess I still have my doubts about your morals ... but I have no doubts about the great person you are and have been to everyone here at Jefferson. You've really added a lot to our school this year- you and your bouncing around ... always smiling ... always laughing and always cheering everyone up. A lot of people are really going to miss you, and one of them that's going to miss you an awful lot is me. I've said a lot of mean things ... but you know I was only kidding. Having your friendship this year has meant an awful lot to me and I'm sure I'll never, ever forget you. I hope someday you come back to America and fulfill your dreams of becoming a doctor- just talking to you and having you understand could cure many people, man.

"Thanks for everything you've given me this year, including a lot of trouble in Trig class. I was very fortunate to get to sit in front of you even though I had to sit in the corner for a few days! Take care and be good; at least try. I hope you accomplish everything you've ever dreamed of and much more. All my love, Barbie '73. The little junior with all the seniors."

I met Barb Feeman once in Alexandria when I returned as a pre-med student at Gustavus Adolphus College in 1974.

I have to bring this signature by Brenda, who was pregnant with her first child and was a senior at Jefferson. She wrote:

"Dear Kwame, thank you for such a wonderful year. You made our class something special. I hope that you'll always remember your new friends in Alexandria. I know that we will always remember you. Always be yourself, and I know that your future plans will come true. Keep smiling because you have such a groovy smile. Love Brenda (Mrs. _____)."

My American mother's signature had a prophetic tone. Here it goes:

"Dearest Kwame, we've been so fortunate to have you for 'our son.' You fit into our family so perfectly and easily. We've had so many good laughs and never any trouble. We love you and will always keep in touch. I know the time will go fast and we'll be together again. Our home will always be your home. Always remember this Bible passage: 'I can do all things through Christ who strengtheneth me.' You'll become a doctor, I know, and a good one. Loads of Love, Mom and Dad Aga."

It is Jesus who has strengthened me in the past thirty-five years of psychotic relapses.

Here is something from a boy:

"Kwame, groovy man! Good luck running at Montevideo. Run groovy, man. I'll let you have all the groovy chicks writing in your book. I'll see you this summer before you go and we'll find some groovy chicks, okay, man? Good luck, Kwame. Rick Banke."

Dear reader, if I say I'll write everything, I surely will bore you but, God willing, I'll have my yearbook available to anyone who wants to read the very many signatures by these wonderful students of Jefferson Senior High School, Alexandria, Minnesota.

When school was finally over, we, the seniors, went through graduation ceremonies with all the academic gown and mortarboard and ribbon. I got my first academic certificate of any kind: an American high school diploma. I was happy indeed.

When finally, I left Alexandria for Africa, my dad wrote in his "Under My Hat" column of the Friday, July 7, 1972, edition of the <u>Lake Region Press</u>:

Our A.F.S. son, Kwame, from Ghana, has started his long trip back home. It all happened early Wednesday morning at Long Prairie where some fifty or more A.F.S. students said goodbye to their American parents, brothers and sisters. And believe me, it was a wet occasion! Tears steadily fell as the goodbyes were said ... and I'll admit I added a few. Kwame had promised no tears and sadness for the farewell ... and he held up like a man though his lips quivered when he stepped on the bus ... turned and then gave us that last beautiful smile. So comes an end to one of the most rewarding experiences our family has been through. Kwame now goes on a two-week tour of the East ... then to Kennedy Airport to board the plane back to Ghana. At home, the A.F.S. will arrange for a family meeting on arrival, then they will hold students for two days of return indoctrination. This is very important, for as difficult as it is for the students to come here and change to our ways, it's twice as hard for them to return home and pick up where they left off a year ago. After two days of intensive orientation and training, then it's home for big family reunions and the beginning of the long tales about their American experiences. So, the first part is over. We have definite plans to have Kwame back, for he wants to be a doctor. And we hope that after his mandatory two years at home, he'll be back as a student at the University of Minnesota.

"We are hooked on the A.F.S. bit now, for we feel it's one of the best things we have going for a better understanding among the nations and the world. You would, too, if you'd give it a try. Anyway, Kwame is gone. We miss him and love him very much. His beautiful black face and ever-white smile has made our lives more meaningful. But gee … the parting is rough."

I received the above clip in Ghana when Mom wrote to me in September 1972 at Cape Coast.

When we left Long Prairie, I sat on the same seats with Geny, and we got to New York the next day. I stayed with a medical professor and his family in Manhattan. They took me on a tour of New York where we took a sailboat to Staten Island to see the Statue of Liberty. On July 18, 1972, I boarded the Pan Am Boeing 747 with many other African foreign students and I arrived in Accra in the early evening, safe and sound, but fatigued.

That was the end of my first year outside my country and, to say it lightly, it was a year of a difference incomparable to any year of my life and I've traveled to the United States four times after this.

Chapter XIII

Back to Ghana, Africa. 1972

It was a good, warm, sun-shiny day in Accra. White, pregnant clouds whisked across the deep blue sky as they danced in a torpor of cumulus bedlam. Wherever the cumulus clouds covered the face of the radiant sun, a shade brought with it a cool comfort of limited life span. However, the defiant sun shone again and brought its perennial African stifling heat.

Some of our girls had gained weight in America. I was as trim and athletic as the precision-wrought statue, David, by Michaelangelo. Two days in Accra was a long time. I wanted to see my parents and brothers and sisters. I had missed them. And I wanted to be back at St. Augustine's quickly. I was in a state of pervasive disquietude.

Selma Alhassan broke my anxiety with a compassionate question in anticipation of a response full of exotic and luxuriant magnificence about my part of the United States.

"Hi, Kwame, how was the Midwest?"

"Minnesota epitomizes the Midwest. The vegetation is emerald green, and there are ubiquitous aqua blue lakes which get their tint from the wide expanse of sapphire skies. The fauna burst with vibrant life and the people are mostly blond, rustic, and merry. At least that describes where I was," I said and smiled a toothful with open, contented mirth.

"Wow, I see you liked it."

"Of course, I did. Didn't you like your stay?'

"Yes, I did like it too."

Mary Anne joined us. "Hi, Kwame. Hi, Selma."

"Hi, Mary Anne," Selma and I said in unison.

"You look nice, Mary Anne," Selma was quick to remark.

"Thanks."

Actually, Mary Anne had gained weight slightly and her cheeks were full. Her eyes shone with radiance.

"Selma, I visited Kwame in his town in Minnesota. It was a really cold affair, but I enjoyed seeing my own countryman once again in that distant land."

"Did you two actually meet?" she asked with deliberate emphasis.

"Yes, I was even at Mary Anne's house for a weekend," I said.

"Wow, I wish I had somebody that close to me."

"Do you go back to Achimota, Selma?" I asked.

"Yes, I wouldn't change schools for a million dollars."

"I am going back to Wesley Girls definitely. I did well in the G.C.E. exams," Mary Anne said.

"According to my headmaster, I topped my class in the ordinary levels missing distinction by a mere point. I don't want to repeat my class as all of you are going to do," I said, full of grandiose hopes.

"What are you going to do? Do you mean you are going to take the two-year advanced level course in one year?"

"Yes."

"You must be crazy," Mary Anne said enviously.

"I will convince and persuade my headmaster to allow me to try," I said and chortled quite carelessly; oblivious of the trauma that lay in wait for me should I fail to pass the sixth upper examination in June 1973. I was going to take advanced pre-university courses in physics, chemistry, biology, and general paper. It was a completely foolhardy decision on my part which the headmaster, Mr. Seddoh, prompty agreed to. He just couldn't hurt the feelings of newly popular Kwame when I wrote him from Minnesota.

"Why are you in so much hurry?" Selma asked.

"I guess I want to get it over with. Moreover, I am not going to sit in the same class with my juniors for some smart guy to beat my excellent academic record."

As we talked, Emmanuel Yamusah, who had been eavesdropping, joined us.

"Kwame, it is dumb. Just go to lower sixth," he said.

"I have decided and I'm going to carry my decision out," I said, every bit as stubborn as ever.

As we talked, we heard a bell and we all walked to the dining hall for supper. I ate sparingly and drank more warm Coke I had brought with me from America. After supper, I talked to Joe Lartey and others for a while and retired to bed to confront my provocative jet-lag. Soon, I dozed off and slept well. In the morning, some parents started arriving at our place of disorientation. Selma's mother came in a Mercedes Benz. I felt like a midget in front of them since I came from a very poor family. I knew my parents would come in very humble clothing and, of course, without a car.

Selma's mother, Mrs. Susanna Alhassan, was the first African woman to hold a cabinet portfolio in Kwame Nkrumah's government in the first republic of Ghana. She was a former deputy minister of education; and, finally, Kwame Nkrumah named her as his minister of Social Welfare and Community Development in 1965. This made her the first woman minister in independent Black Africa. This appointment actually set a precedent that's been carried on in Ghana and many other nations ever since. So, that was the exquisite historical aura that hovered around Selma and her family. No wonder I courted and lost her friendship. She was highborn. She got her things together and that was the last time I saw her until I returned from the United States in 1983, bought a black and white TV, and found her as the main television newscaster whose innate African beauty was on the lips of every TV watcher in Ghana.

My folks came in the afternoon after traveling for four hours on the Government Transport bus. They were very happy to see me and I was very happy too. I introduced them to the remaining friends and I could see my father exulting in a dignified proud integrity. My mother had not gone to school, so she didn't understand what we were talking about, as Papa insisted we spoke in English. I think he was trying to see if I had picked up the likeable American accent. He said I did, and I guess I was full of contentment for that compliment.

"Okay, Kwame, let's go. It's getting late."

"I'll get my suitcase and carry-on bag."

As I did so, Papa was explaining excitedly things to my mother. She kept nodding, saying, "Un-huh," and smiling gleefully. She was really proud of her son indeed.

We took a taxi back to the Transport Station and boarded a Kumasi-bound bus, which brought us to the city in a little less than four hours. I was tired, but I didn't sleep and I was mesmerized by the stark contrast of where I had been and here. I just couldn't imagine the comparison from the skyscrapers of the Empire State Building, World Trade Centers, and the amazing New York skyline and the Brooklyn Bridge to the red brick adobe houses with thatch and a serpentine and pot-holed two-lane Kumasi-Accra trunk road. Hmmn! Something indeed!

"We are far behind, Papa."

"Rome was not built in a day."

"Before we become like them, they'll be building skyscrapers on the moon."

"Don't worry. We will get there someday," Papa said, full of distant optimism.

I showed some postcards of New York and Minneapolis, and Papa soon appreciated what I had been saying. He passed the pictures on to my mother and, in her rustic upbringing at Anomabo, she was definitely hypnotized by them.

"Is this where you went, Kwame?" she asked me in Fanti.

"Yes," I said.

"Shieee, the place is beautiful," she said and hugged my shoulders. I could see she was radiating in enormous pride.

My nine brothers and sisters were joyous at my arrival. Papa had bought all of them new <u>Buroni Wawu</u> (second-hand clothes) and they looked good and cheerful.

Adwoa took my suitcase and I handed my carry-on bag to Kofi as he gently took it from my shoulder. The mud compound had been swept clean and the kitchen opposite the house had been white-washed. The gutter on the road in front of the house had been desilted and all the <u>ankore</u>, or water barrels, had been filled with water. I entered our two-room chamber and hall and Papa had taken away the old blue cushion covers and replaced them with new white calico covers. I could see that even the very old antique furniture had been polished. There were new <u>Buroni Wawu</u> curtains to match the new cushion covers.

When I entered the chamber where my father's bed was, our black and white TV was still there. It was covered on top by a calico shawl and the new addition to the room was a table fan with blue blades. Papa put it on for me. I felt cooled, for I was sweating already.

Sitting down finally, my mother brought me a calabash full of water to formally welcome me back. All my brothers and sisters were crowded in the small room and there was standing room only. Papa started with the amanee. He said, "Everything has been smooth-sailing since you left, the same way you left us, the same way we are now. You come from the distant lands of the white person. Give your amanee."

"Yes, Kwame, what is the news from the white man?" my mother added. All my brothers and sisters were smiling.

I smiled too and started by saying, "As you know, it is exactly a year ago since I left you. When Papa and Maame saw me off at Kotoka International Airport, I boarded the big plane (my first time) to join many teenagers from all over Africa. Some of the Africans were white people from South Africa, North and Southern Rhodesia. As everything was new to me, I was very quiet, almost shy. Flying in a plane was a different and unique experience, but soon I was already tired of it since the journey between here and the white man's country is far indeed. We landed in one African country for about an hour and finally touched down in New York, a big city in America, in the early evening. It was a big change because all the buildings were very tall, the roads had as many as four lanes for cars going in one direction, and by night there were neon, fluorescent, and incandescent lights. I traveled in air-conditioned long buses to a certain college called C.W. Post."

"Were the buses really air conditioned?" Esi asked, quite amazed.

"Yes, that place is America, you know."

"Did you get fufu to eat?" Naana asked absentmindedly.

"No, there's no fufu in America. We had their own food. They called them hamburgers and hot dogs. We washed them down with a glass of soda or a milkshake."

"Were they delicious, and did you like them?"

"Yes, Kofi. It is something like bread with fried ground beef inside and, you know the white man, he likes green things, so there were what they call 'lettuce' and pickles also. They put something like tomato sauce called 'ketchup' on it, and I tell you, it was delicious."

"Nice," my sisters said and laughed. My parents were smiling and very intent on hearing more.

"You want to hear more?"

"Yes!" thrilled, they all smiled childlike and said in a loud voice. Silence ensued. I began again:

"There were many shops and restaurants and cars. You know in America no one walks."

"Really?"

"Yes."

In a couple of breathless moments when nobody dared interrupt my story, I coughed and continued:

"In New York, I didn't see that much green vegetation. Most of the land is replaced with concrete and enormously tall buildings called skyscrapers, which always cast shadows on the earth far away beneath them. In the buildings wherever we went, we took lifts. They call them 'elevators'. In most of the big shops, there were sliding staircases they called escalators. You didn't need to walk if you didn't want to. You just stood on one of these escalators and it would take you wherever you wanted to go.

"One thing that I found very interesting were the 'machine salespeople.' They called them 'vending machines.' No one tended them, but if you wanted to buy something, you just put in the correct number of coins, and when you press a button, your item will come down in an opening for you to take. Sometimes a sign will light up and say, 'THANK YOU.'"

"Wow, very interesting, very interesting indeed," Naana and my mother said.

"Shiee <u>Aburokyire</u>. Kwesi Buronyi is wonderful," Araba said, quite astonished.

"Wait, I haven't finished. Just by this vending machine is also a change machine which will give you change for a dollar or five dollars if you put the paper money in it."

"Really?" Adwoa said, wide-mouthed.

I was going to give more installments of my experience, when we heard knocking on the hall door. When my mother went there to open it, it was Mr. Ampah and his wife who had come to welcome me back home.

"Hello, Kwame. Akwaaba," Mr. Ampah said.

"Thank you."

"How is my white master?" Mrs. Ampah said.

"I am just fine, thank you."

My mother told my brothers and sisters to leave to make room for the visitors. They were disappointed, but obeyed immediately and got out without complaining. Mr. Ampah and family took the seats.

"Can I bring you some water?" my mother asked.

"No, thanks; we just ate," Mrs. Ampah said.

"Kwame was telling us about the first day he arrived in America," Papa said.

"Oh, our white man, what was the most different things you saw and experienced?" Mr. Ampah asked, quite anxious to hear descriptions of exotic sights and stuff.

"The most interesting things I experienced were the seasons. There were four distinct seasons, and each one of them was so different."

"Tell us more," my mother said.

"When I got there the first time, it was what they call 'summer.' Summer is just like here right now- hot, sometimes humid too. The trees are all green and, occasionally, it rains heavily. The crops grow well in summer."

"What do the people like to do in summer?" Papa was quick to ask.

"They continue to work, of course. But most of them take summer vacations to go to beaches, resort areas on lakes, go hiking, fishing, or rock climbing."

"What is the next season, which is much different from ours?" Mrs. Ampah asked.

"From summer, we go to a season the Americans call 'fall.' It is very beautiful because most leaves on some trees change color from green to bright red, yellow, and brown. Together with the green leaves the colors make the environment exciting and very beautiful indeed."

"Hmmn!" Mrs. Ampah and my mother said.

"You see, after some time, the leaves all fall to the gound. That's maybe why they call it fall, because the leaves fall from the trees."

"Really?" Papa asked.

"Yes."

"Do the plants die then without their leaves?"

"Not necessarily. They just stand bare through the very cold season they call 'winter.'"

"Yes, tell us about winter. I hear it is very, very cold," Papa said as Mr. Ampah nodded.

"It starts getting cold almost in the middle of October, but that is not even winter. Winter is supposed to start in December. At this time, the biggest change is that the earth is covered with a carpet of white stuff called snow. It is very cold indeed and soon turns to ice. You know, where I was, the lakes even froze to hard ice and cars and people could go over a lake because it is frozen."

"Doesn't the ice break? Isn't it dangerous for them?" Papa asked.

"At most times the ice is very thick. Ice can be as hard as a rock. When you drink ice water, you think it is cold, but where I was, it was colder than inside the fridge. Sometimes when you spit in winter, by the time the spit falls to the ground, it is all ice."

"Hmm ... really?" they all said.

"Sometimes too when a person cries, the tears freeze on his face."

"Oh, no, Kwame. As for this you're pulling our legs!" Papa said, looked at Mr. Ampah and laughed. Mrs. Ampah sat open-mouthed in complete astonishment. My mother was also laughing and nodding her head slowly in accompaniment.

"How do the people live. Don't they freeze to death?"

"No, I am not dead! The homes and all other buildings are heated. However, when you go outside, you must be well dressed in woolen coats, you must cover you head with a woolen cap or hat, you must wear a scarf, and wear warm gloves and warm boots."

"I wouldn't want to go abroad because of the cold weather," Mrs. Ampah said.

"I don't blame you. The white man himself actually doesn't like it, but he has no other choice."

"That's why my grandfather said they used to come and live in Africa," Mr. Ampah said, as he made a point about the white man's historical exploration and colonialism in Africa.

"Where do they get their food when it is so cold? I know crops won't grow!" Papa asked.

"Yes, where?" Mrs. Ampah added.

"Oh, America is a big place. While it is cold in one place, other places too such as Florida, Texas, Arizona, etc. are warm, and they grow the fresh vegetables. But during the warm months, the soy beans, wheat, oats, and corn are grown and harvested. So they have plenty in stock."

"Where are all the animals at this time? The cow, the goats, sheep and horses. What do they eat if the ground is covered with ice?" my mother, very curious indeed, asked.

"During the warm months, the farmers work very hard to cut grass, alfalfa, and clover and make them into bales and stack them. They call this hay. The grass dries out and that's what the animals eat in winter. They are also given grain too. Oh, yes, they are kept in heated sheds otherwise, they'll freeze to death."

"Poor animals," mother said.

"Okay, you said there were four seasons. What is the last one?" Mrs. Ampah asked.

"The last one is spring. It is quite wet then because all the snow and ice melt, and it rains too. The plants start to grow back leaves and soon everywhere is green. The farmers go to the fields to plough and sow. Most Americans like spring because by that time they are very tired of the cold winter, but I like fall the best."

"Very interesting indeed. If my son had not gone to the white man's land to get a firsthand experience, we surely wouldn't be hearing this." Papa said, very proud indeed.

"True," Mr. Ampah said and nodded. My mother and Mrs. Ampah nodded too, and continued to nod, seemingly having learned a lot about the white man's land.

"America is not just for the white man. There are black people there too."

"Oh, yes, the slaves," Mrs. Ampah said.

"They are no longer slaves. They became free a long time ago, but compared to the whites, they are poorer. You hear about them mostly in music and sports."

I remember at college how we learned about slaves and their horrendous ordeal, especially in the Middle Passage, where our ancestors were forced to lie in their defecation and vomit while chained, and where most of the women and children lost their innocence again and again to white sailors. It didn't matter whether they had been impregnated or infected with white man's diseases like syphillis or gonorrhea. And it didn't matter whether the impregnated women's children were born black. They also became slaves. The white man enslaved his own children because they had part of the black blood in them.

"Our ancestors suffered a lot," Maame said.

"Yes, they still suffer because racism and discrimination will not go away in a highly civilized country like America."

"It's a big shame," Mr. Ampah said.

"In the 1960s, I saw with my own eyes on TV how the blacks were hosed down and chased with fierce German Shepherds by whites just because blacks were denied civil rights and they were fighting for them. We all watched with terrible dismay when President Kennedy, Bobby Kennedy, Martin Luther King and Malcolm X were all shot and killed. These people were fighting for blacks in America."

"We have learned a lot from our white master but I think he is worn out," Papa said.

"Yes, he is," my mother said.

"Okay, we'll leave, but we will come back to hear more stuff later. Welcome back again." Mr. Ampah said.

"Yes, welcome back," Mrs. Ampah said and they got up to leave.

"Bye," Papa and Maame said.

I felt I needed to go to the bathroom and toilet, and I was appalled because there wasn't a toilet in our house. We all patronized the communal public toilet about a hundred yards away from the house. This is what I detested most about my coming back to Ghana after getting used to the nice and clean water closet of the Americans.

Usually, the latrine boys cleaned the latrines, but when the public was unfortunate enough to use the latrines when the latrine boys went on strike, then the toilet was abhorrently filthy. Because people defecated anywhere, there were feared incidences of diseases like cholera, and also the smells were obnoxious.

I came out from the room and used the bathroom outside to urinate. My brother, Naana, accompanied me to the toilet. Luckily, it was clean and when I was done with my session, and used my left hand and a newspaper to wipe myself, we returned to the house after saying hello to a neighbor.

It was supper time. My mother had deliberately cooked two meals of fufu and chicken peanut soup, and Jollof rice with meaty chunks of beef in it. I was served both, and Maame bought a ten-pesewa-worth of ice water for me. It was good to eat fufu and rice again. I relished the delectably exquisite taste of Maame's cooking and I knew, yeah, I was really back to Africa. The hot peppers in the soup smarted but with the ice water, I was fine.

That night it was steamy hot. I kept sweating. Papa kindly brought the fan to the hall where I slept with my brothers and sisters on mats strewn on the floor. After we watched "Osofo Dadzie," in which O.D. and Kojo Kwakye were at their buffoonery best with quizzical good humor, I retired to bed to soothe my jet lag which was still there.

Chapter XIV

Back in Ghana and Advanced Level
Education 1972 and 1973

Family life was not hard to adjust to. I had become a very popular guy by going abroad. People acknowledged my presence and gave me special treatment. My friends came to my house to play ping pong, listen to conversation from the distant lands, and, best of all, look at my color photographs taken with white people. They just couldn't imagine my privilege because at that time there was no color photography in Ghana. Some of my friends wanted copies of photographs to decorate their albums because they were colored. If I didn't give them to them, they tried to swipe them.

What impressed them the most was my school yearbook and newspaper clippings and articles about me in the <u>Alexandria</u> <u>Press</u>. They all looked at me as the young ambassador. My parents were the proudest people whenever visitors came to our house.

I had brought a walkie-talkie given to me by Mr. Aga. Being totally novel to my father, he'd deliberately give a set to my mother in the kitchen and they'd communicate in the presence of the astonished visitors. Some of my friends begged my father to let them use the walkie-talkie, but Papa would not let them for fear that someone would eventually steal them or they wouldn't know how to use them and break them. He always played it safe.

My friends thought my demeanor and comportment, my speech and American accent, and my wearing jeans and other better clothes made me very refined indeed. They all vowed to struggle to come to the United States someday. Most of my friends were from St. Paul's Roman Catholic Elementary School and were in secondary school. They were among the brightest students in the country. Richard Okine, a Ph.D. graduate of M.I.T. and a duPont engineer living in Delaware, had topped the whole country in the G.C.E. ordinary level in 1971. He was a student of Opoku Ware Secondary School and got all ones in his seven subjects. Kwame Dangerous was a graduate of Brown University. Dr. Francis Dickson got a medical degree from Howard. Dr. Charles Borromeo Kankam got first class at Kwame Nkrumah University of Science and Technology and went to Imperial College in Britain for his Ph.D. in Civil Engineering. Dr. Bucknor (a treasurer at the African Development Bank) also studied in the United States. Mr. Brew Hammond got an M.S. degree from Canada, and Francis T. Oduro is a lecturer at the University of Science and Technology, Kumasi, a Ph.D. candidate in Physics.

While we were still teenagers, we were studious, academically very competitive and avid athletes in both track and field and soccer. I was the best in table tennis besides being a four hundred meter track star.

We were high spirited and anxious to get back to school in September of 1972. When September finally came, I went to Cape Coast, where I was still very popular. People were fascinated about my glasses, which got darker in sunlight and lighter indoors (glasses with photogray lenses). They admired my blue jeans. Some said I had grown taller and gained weight, although I hadn't. Some students always spoke English to me, even if they were my tribesmen, to get a glimpse of my American accent. Sometimes, I tried to overplay it to impress them, and my newspaper clippings were posted on the school notice board for everyone to see and read.

I won many trophies, ribbons, certificates and medals in America, and all were displayed. I donated the trophies to the headmaster, who displayed them in his office, and used them as trophies during the annual Inter-House Althletic Competition.

I played basketball and tennis with Kwesi Yorke, now Dr. Kwesi Nduom, Ghana's Minister of Energy in the Kuffuor's Government (the first A.F.S. student at Wisconsin) on the school tennis courts. Somehow, girls from Holy Child got my address and wrote me fan letters.

Mr. Seddoh (our headmaster) said he'd let me be in upper sixth, but he wished greatly that I would go to lower sixth, where I would be the automatic senior prefect without student election. I declined to be in lower sixth.

I stayed in upper sixth, and started a tough and tedious study in physics, chemistry, and biology. I did most of the studying on my own because I had received no instruction from my teachers. I copied notes from friends, and really I was unconsciously wearing myself out. I lucubrated most times and got the appellation "Nocturnal Bookworm" and a "Miner." At the same time too, I was in sports training hard. They all wanted to watch the guy from America run.

I did very well at the Inter-House Athletic Competition and became the best runner in the Central Region at the Later Collegiate Athletic Competition. I remember Mary Anne came to speak and congratulate me at the 1973 competition after I had won the four hundred meters.

When I came back to Kumasi for vacation, I trained at the Kumasi International Sports Stadium with Mr. Lawson and Richard Okine.

The year was progressing very fast and the academic work was gruesome for me. But who was really rushing me to give myself such punishment? Finally, the G.C.E. advanced level examinations was taken. I realized my mistake. It was tough indeed. I spent the long vacation full of anxiety and waiting for my results; and when they finally came, I was shocked. I got a flat F in physics, subsidiaries in biology and chemistry, and a B in general paper. Those results meant I was out of academic life in Ghana. I had to wait one year and take the exams again on my own. It was traumatic because I thought, as bright as I was, I could never fail an examination; and you know, in Ghana, for a bright student to fail an examination, especially the G.C.E., is very shameful.

I did not know how to divulge the news of my results to my parents, especially my father. I felt extremely ashamed and defeated.

The Ashantis and Fantis have a proverb which goes, "Wise and good counsel never changes a person, except when painful adversity strikes."

I saw the validity of the proverb, because here I was in painful shame and not knowing what to do. I consulted some friends, who advised me not to give up, but rather take a private night school course at the Adult Education Institute at Asem Elementary School in Kumasi to improve my grades to qualify to go to the university.

"What have I put myself into?" I was ashamed to meet my friends. I stayed indoors most of the time. My parents were worried ,but they didn't cease to encourage me to register at the Adult Education Institute for my remedials.

"Don't be so dejected, Kwame," Papa would say.

"The world doesn't end for you with one failure in life. Life is not all successes, if you haven't learned that by now," my mother, who sympathized with my sudden plunge from grace to grass, would always say to encourage me.

I registered and studied my advanced level science courses again. Sometimes, I couldn't do any laboratory class at Opoku Ware because the science teachers were always absent as their remuneration was very little.

After a painful study all year, my father paid my examination fee and I took all the tests again. I was satisfied because I knew I had done well. All the year in 1973-74, I was corresponding with my American father, Mr. Aga. I told him my problems and he, in turn, using my excellent high school grades at Jefferson, sought and found admission and a scholarship at Gustavus Adolphus College for me. Mr. Aga paid for my deluxe trip, which included a helicopter flight from Kennedy Airport to LaGuardia, and on to a Northwest Airline bound for Minneapolis, Minnesota.

I got back to the United States on August 7, 1974, to start college at St. Peter in Gustavus Adolphus College. I was definitely glad and relieved that at least I had a chance to continue my education. I have already told you about what happened to me as a freshman at Gustavus Adolphus College in the beginning of this book. I developed mental illness almost a couple of weeks after my freshman year. I didn't know how to deal with this overwhelming adversity. However, with the college acting in '*loco parentis*' and, with the strong help of my white father Mr. Aga, I was able to make it.

Chapter XV

*Years at Gustavus Adolphus College, St.
Peter Minnesota, 1974-1979*

I looked at myself and kept asking God questions. Here I was: I never smoked cigarettes or marijuana, neither had I ever done any drugs like cocaine, crack, L.S.D., or heroin, was a complete teetotaler, and I had never had sex yet. I was a straight guy with impeccable old-world-African-Catholic morals, but it was I who had to lose my mind. I kept asking God:

"Why me? Life is not fair, Lord."

I never understood why but, recently, I think God is giving the answer, and I just thank Him for making me sick and burdening me with my cross- a yoke that I laid to rest on Jesus Christ who saved me, for I wouldn't have known God if I hadn't been sick. Could you believe that I had such a tough social life at Gustavus Adolphus College with all the so-called sane people? I never had a single date at Gustavus. Many times, I looked forward to getting sick so that I could be sent to St. Peter State Hospital where I had made friends with the patients and nurses and Dr. Bohrud. There, I was accepted and found solace, compassion and comfort in the 'cukoo's nest.'

I spent a lot of my four academic years at Gustavus Adolphus, St. Peter sick in the hospital. What was cracking me up in America? The doctor said it could be hereditary, explaining something about genetic disintegration or mutation at some point with my father's and mother's genes. Now, though, I don't believe all these. People don't understand mental illness and

I believe even the best psychiatrists don't. Some of them never experienced psychosis of any kind. As an African who has not yet found a cure for my chronic bouts, I retreat to the age-old African belief in superstition. I believe sincerely that witchcraft has a predisposing factor in the causation of my illness and those of my brothers and sisters. So, whether science will say it is lack of Dopamine, Serotonin or Norepinephrine in my brain cells, I don't believe the scientists because why the recurring episodes if the medications I was taking were supplying these chemicals.

Listen, when I returned to Africa in 1983, I discovered that all the ten brothers and sisters of my parents were sick with some major debasing mental illness or some other type of problem. My father, now dead, was never sick and my mother never had any mental illness. No one that I know in my extended family has an incidence of mental illness, but look all my ten brothers and sisters; yes, all ten of us were sick.

My elder brother, now long dead, was a grand-mal epileptic. He died at 21 after a disgraceful life-long struggle with the damned illness. I never understood why my brother should suffer so much when he had seizures. I was so terrified of them. When he had them, he knocked his head several times against the hard floor, soiled himself with micturition and defecation, foamed at the mouth, and passed out, period. He always had to sleep off the pain but more pain and shame awaited him when he woke up, for he was all cut up in the face and head and badly bruised.

My next brother after him is what I call a kleptomaniac. He will steal for the mere fun of it. He can never hold a job, and doesn't care at all about his intelligent and only child. He loves marijuana, booze, and women.

You wouldn't believe it, but my sister joined her husband in London, and all of a sudden became a schizophrenic. She had four children, is, of course, divorced, and now has fibroids and is roaming the streets of Amakom, Kumasi, Ghana. Unfortunately, she died suddenly about a year ago.

Next comes myself. I came to college in America in 1974, and all of a sudden cracked up with manic-depressive psychosis. I was a brilliant student, the only member of my extended family past or present who went to college and graduate school. I've had 20 relapses in 35 years and really suffered a lot.

You guessed it. My brother after me was an epileptic. However, he was lucky. He was healed by a spiritual church leader and is now doing very well as a business executive in the capital of my country. He bought me my plane ticket, and has built four houses, has a Mercedes, a Toyota Sequoia, and an Infinity.

Next, comes my sister, a once beautiful light complexioned girl with two children and divorced. She never had a job, and has been in Nigeria to stay for several years. One wonders what happens to her there. My sister after her never married, but has two kids whom she doesn't look after. She works in a hotel in Accra and is wild indeed. My brother after her is a prominent person at his job. Once, I cried because when I visited him and we were sleeping, he was shouting in his sleep having nightmares. He felt ashamed when he woke up and explained that some terrifying being was chasing him with a dagger and about to stab him. Maybe having nightmares is not, necessarily, a serious mental problem, but could it be a witch chasing him in the dream? He gave me a thousand dollars to use as pocket money when I was coming to the United States this time.

My brother after him is also a wee (marijuana) smoking kleptomaniac. He has been out of sight and somewhere at Obuasi. No one knows where he is. He stole my business executive brother's expensive video cassette player and sold it cheaply.

Then my last brother, an intelligent guy who never succeeded to pass an examination, didn't care what he would be in the future, had very low self-esteen, and worked as a construction laborer at Accra. He finally died of a suicide recently. He left a note that he was utterly dissatisfied with the albatrosses of real life.

Now, dear reader, you tell me if there aren't some evil and bad witches who don't want any of my brothers and sisters, including myself, to succeed in life. Anyway, supersitition is basically speculation, so we leave everything to God who is omniscient.

Now back to Gustavus Adolphus College in 1975. Because I was very lonely, rejected, lovesick, and never could find a date with the sane girls, I became depressed and cracked up again. This time the school officials had a good reason to kick me out of college and send me back to Ghana. When I heard about their decision, I was very sad indeed because I knew that if they sent me to Ghana, I would be ostracized and never make it in life, because in Africa, lunatics are really despised and shunned. Let me give you a picture of an African madman in Kejetia, Kumasi, Ghana. He is usually naked, abhorrently dirty with matted, dusty hair, doesn't have a home (ostracized), roams about and sleeps anywhere, even in the mud when it is raining. He eats from the dirty gutters and garbage dumps and is completely out of it in life.

After I had had treatment at St. Peter State Hospital, I went back to college and knew about the plans of the school authorities. I didn't know what to do, but I was lucky because God, being so good, always cares for the children He loves. I told my roommate Mark. You remember him from Chapter I. Mark didn't hesitate and called his parents in St. Paul. The next day, they were on the college campus to meet the school authorities. They were able to avert my dangerous plight and succeeded and convinced the authorities to let me stay and study. I had only one day left to fly to New York with Dave Wicklund, our school registrar, to see me board a plane to Africa.

Now, tell me it wasn't God working miracles through good people like the Halvorsons. I kept cracking up, being rejected, and being lovesick, but studying hard and being the only black student on the Dean's List at Gustavus, until June 1979, when I graduated with two concurrent degrees in biology and classics (my professors I remember most at Gustavus were Dr. and Dr. (Mrs.) Freiert, for they always, out of their own volition, came to St. Peter State Hospital often to give me classes in Latin, Greek, and Classical Civilization. God bless them). When I applied to graduate school, I got admission and teaching assistantships at the Ohio State University and University of Louisiana, Baton Rouge in classics. I chose to go to Ohio State as fate would have it, and now I am very glad I chose the university of James Thurber and Jessie Owens.

I arrived on the university campus in September to start my graduate work in classics. During the first quarter, I enjoyed Lucretius in Latin, but found Herodotus in Classical Greek to be very demanding and difficult. I realized I didn't have enough preparation in Greek because graduate work in Greek demanded very precise translations and I couldn't handle them. I studied Virgil, Horace, Juvenal, Ovid, Livy, and Philoctetes. I always burned the midnight candle. I tried harder and harder.

In 1980, I got a telephone call from my half sister in Rhode Island that our father had died suddenly in Kumasi, Ghana. I had to go to Africa for the funeral so, I paid for a return trip ticket after I had obtained a two-week leave of absence from the authorities at Ohio State.

When I got to Kumasi, my father had already been buried. I felt very bad indeed, because 1974 was the last time I saw him, and I had written to tell him about my plight in the United States and he wished greatly to see me. I returned to find out that the Classics Department wanted to take back the teaching assistantship. One day, Professor Davis and Professor Mark Morford called me and divulged their decision to me. I was shattered, not knowing what to do.

Luckily, the Black Studies Department was just across the hall from the Classics Department in the Humanities Building. I walked in there and sought admission and a teaching assistantship. Upon perusing my background, I was offered both. Does God work wonders for His children? I say a big "Yes," because He was always there to save me when I encountered big problems. I prayed a simple prayer to thank Him.

I had finally come into contact with several black people in the United States. I found the black student to be a very proud person to have chance at college education. At that time the black population on campus was insignificant compared to the 55 thousand strong college population.

I felt kind of bad for the black American. I found that blacks died a long time ago, and hadn't resurrected yet. The white man has not helped him by stripping him of his culture and language and superimposing upon him his culture and English cultural imperialism. Even then, they said most blacks spoke Black English Vernacular or Ebonics. Anybody without a culture is dead.

The black person in America is the biggest minority in the country, yet even the language of the Latinos, Spanish, is spoken and taught in schools. Has the black American considered pressing for the teaching of an African language like Hausa or Swahili in schools in America? It could give some poor African teachers jobs here, but then the black Americans will have an indigenous language to be proud of. Interesting indeed, and I wish the African Americans would think about it. Also, go to Ghana for African language lore, because if you go there, the first thing you'll realize is that our rich language is advertised even on cars, buses, and trucks. Consider these, written on many vehicles:

"Nyame Na W'aye" - It is the Lord who has done this

"Nyame Ye Odo" - God is love

"Allahu Akbar" - The Lord, the Merciful

"Aquai Allah" - There's God

"Allah Baamu Lafia" - God strengthens

"Wiase Ye Sum" - The world is dark

"Dwen Hwe Kan" - Think about the future

"Odo Ye Wu" - Love is unto death and so on and so forth.

Somebody finally took my love bait. I had been very lovesick at Gustavus. I sat with this girl in one of my Black Studies classes and mustered enough courage to talk.

"Hi."

"Hi, what's happening?" she said.

"Nothing much really. How about you?"

"Can't complain. You from Africa?"

"Yes, how do you know?"

"Your accent. Where in Africa?"

"Ghana, West Africa."

"What's your name?"

"Kwame."

"What?"

"I said, 'Kwame.' "

"How do you spell it?"

"K-W-A-M-E."

"Oh, that's it. I thought it was Q-U-A ... "

"No, just K-W ... "

"It's different."

"Yes, what's yours?"

"Valencia."

"Really? It's the name of a Spanish Soccer Team. Are you Spanish?"

"A born, bred black American."

"You have a nice voice."

"Thank you. It's only natural."

"Well, that's what I like ... natural!"

"I think you are nice," she said.

"Thank you."

"Do you stay on campus?" she asked.

"No, I stay close to High Street on East Avenue."

"That's where I walk past every morning and evening on my way to school and back. Can I pay you a visit once?"

"No, not so soon!"

"But when?"

"After we go out for a while."

"Thank God! I'm glad you are interested."

"I wouldn't be talking to you if I wasn't."

I heard my heart sink a happy thud. It started a spondaic pulse for I was excited.

"What do you like to do for fun? Movies, dinner, bowling?"

"I like dinner and movies."

"Will you go out with me?"

"Where?"

"Dinner."

"I'll give it a try."

"Thank you. You mind taking the bus? I don't drive."

"I have a car. We can go in mine. When do we go?"

"Today is Wednesday. How about Friday night?"

"That's cool with me."

Valencia agreed to pick me up at 6:30. She was exactly on the dot on Friday night, and I took her to the cafeteria at the Holiday Inn. It might sound fancy, but at graduate school, I always had plenty of money, as I spent 40 dollars a month on food, paid my rent, and saved the rest of my salary. In fact, when I finished graduate school in 1982, I had saved $7,000. I still have the receipt from Bank One, Columbus to show any skeptic.

On our third date, I invited Valencia to my place and she allowed me to be intimate with her. Sex is what you don't get with "sane" people when you are mentally sick. She told me I was inexperienced and a novice. I was embarrassed; but I told her I was ready to learn from her if she was more experienced:

"I'll do whatever you asked me to do."

She agreed, so later, she taught me how to please a woman companionably and sexually. I learned fast and soon; later on, I was giving her orgasms with spastic movements. One night she orgasmed and shed tears. She said I made her happy and those tears were happy ones.

I began to love Valencia with all my heart and even asked her to marry me. However, I received a jolt of my darned illness and Valencia broke my heart.

"I don't want no crazy brother with me." I still remember the rejection and pain of that statement. I kept asking myself, "Will somebody ever love me?" I was starting to feel sorry for myself.

I remember my illness in 1981 very clearly, for it brought upon me the most terrible year of my life. I had been seeing a psychiatrist clandestinely on campus. He was Dr. Svendson. He was a good man, probably not a very good doctor, because he couldn't help me prevent a relapse. I had been taking my Haldol and Lithium as usual and always getting the screen blood tests every week. I was very particular about my medication and still am. However, in the summer, I started having trouble sleeping. I was alarmed, but in my case, if there was going to be an impending episode, nothing could prevent it. It had to happen and be treated. So, bang! I landed at Upham Hall, a psychiatric unit at Ohio State. With my very bad luck, I had not paid my health insurance fee that quarter for some reason.

When the doctor found this out, he wanted to get me out of the hospital real quick, so he prescribed Electro Convulsive Therapy and jolted me with high voltage, E.C.T. through my brain. That was the most wicked thing anybody could do to me because after it, I was in severe amnesia for about one year.

I was put on a table, and each side of my head touched with electric tongs. An electric shock was then administered and my body simulated an epileptic attack. When I regained consciousness, I was in a terrifying state of disorientation. My thoughts were incoherent and I could recall nothing. I had even suddenly forgotten the names of my most intimate friends, including Valencia. Jesus! What was I going to do? I was supposed to use this brain to study. God, whose marvels are never limitless and who always cares for me, Alleluia, saw me through. For, on September 2, 1982, I was among the graduates of 281st commencement at the Ohio State University. I was the proud recipient of a Master of Arts degree in Black Studies. Alleluia, praise the Lord! I still cannot fathom God's greatest miracle for me so far. Was I happy? To be euphemistic, I was happier than an angel.

Chapter XVI

Graduation From Ohio State, Providence, R.I.,
and Ghana, Africa. 1982 and 1983

I called my American father to tell him about it. In four days' time, Dad sent me a check for three hundred dollars to celebrate it. I also wrote to Dr. and Mrs. Loren Halvorson at Arc Retreat Center, Staunchfield, Minnesota to tell them about my success. They happily sent me two hundred dollars. I was really laden with money.

After I got my degree, all of a sudden, I was out of my element. My element was academics. I hadn't lined up a job and I hadn't sought to continue to get a doctorate degree. Actually, I didn't know where to continue on a Black Studies degree. You know, Black Studies was only a recent discipline.

I talked to my half sister, and she asked me to come and stay with her in Rhode Island. At that time, she was living in Pawtucket as a permanent resident- that is, she had a green card. She had also been in the United States for eight years already. Like a pack rat, I packed everything, and boarded a plane to Providence. The East Coast was a big change from the Midwest. Americans, here, talked with a slight accent. And, of course, here, there were several Ashantis and other Ghanaians.

My sister had a three-bedroom apartment, and she lived there with her husband and two kids, one only a couple of weeks old, so she was a nursing mother. She kept open house and overstepped the customary Ghanaian hospitality in America, for Ghanaians, especially the Ashantis, came to the house and sponged on her at any time of the day. They knew that whenever they came, they wouldn't be denied their drink (alcohol or pop), nor food in the form of fufu made from steaming a mixture of potato buds and potato starch. So, as early as six A.M., there were people in the house. I felt uncomfortable because I wasn't used to this in homes in Minnesota and in Ohio.

Some of the Ghanaians, instead of saving their money, used it to pay over-blown telephone bills, which sometimes went up to a 1000 dollars a month. They, arbitrarily, called Europe and Africa at any time of the day and allowed collect calls also from these distant places. The television was turned on from 5:30 A.M. and kept running until midnight, never to be turned off even if nobody was watching and the programs were not good and relevant ... a waste of electricity.

Most of them did menial work as janitors, orderlies, or nurses' aides, and as factory hands since they just couldn't fathom the need to go to school. So there were middle form four leavers and form five graduates of Ghanaian elementary and secondary schools.

There were many gossips and jokes going around in this little Ghanaian community in Rhode Island. There was the gossip of this married man who was unfaithful and went for an American girlfriend, not knowing that she was epileptic. One day, he had bought her dinner and aggressively sought romance. The girl readily agreed. They went to her apartment and started a really hot sex affair. The girl was so filled with complete orgasmic pleasure that, for some reason, it triggered a seizure. The man, obviously frightened, instead of helping her, disengaged himself and ran off without his pants.

There was this person too who worked hard to put a white girl through graduate school with the promise of marriage. After she finished her Master's degree, she called the guy 'a mother-fucking asshole' and left him penniless. In the meantime, ironically, the parents and brothers and sisters of this guy in Ghana were very hard up and eating kenkey without fish and naked fufu without meat- a disgrace.

Also, another person spent all his money on prostitutes. I asked how he compared these prostitutes to Ghanaian girls, and he said Ghanaian girls were better. Then I asked, "Why don't you save all this money and try to bring over a Ghanaian girl who would love you and start a family?"

I always got the same answer, saying, "Ghanaian girls are bad because when they come and realize that it is not all that rosy here, they'll leave you."

That was not true because it was the men who left these unfortunate girls who came over to become single mothers- a real burdensome affair in the United States. When will the Diasporan African male learn to marry?

There was also the gossip of the nurses' aides who were treated unkindly, especially by the old folks, because these old folks called them mother-fucking good-for-nothing African niggers and assholes. These aides said nothing and continued to work patiently because without having gone to school, they were stuck with this low-paying burdensome job. They said the old folks were crazy.

One person also tries to dress very well and spends lavishly on clothes. I heard that one day this Ashanti guy bought a shirt for two thousand dollars and jewelry for six thousand dollars just because people would say, "Akwasi, you look nice." Absolute folly indeed and a total waste of resources which could go a along way to improve lives in Ghana.

At that time, President Reagan had just come to power after defeating the incumbent, President Jimmy Carter, against the backdrop of the Iran Hostage Affair. Reagan was a no-nonsense president, for he fired all the air traffic controllers when they went on strike. Later too, he bombed Tripoli and Benghazi in Gaddaffi's Libya because Gaddaffi, he claimed, was perpetuating international terrorism. Anyway, at the commencement of his leadership term, the economy in America was very bad and in a recession. I spent a whole year going to the Rhode Island Employment Center to find a job and didn't get one.

Finally, a Ghanaian friend said there was an opening for an "aprapra" (janitorial) job at his workplace, Arden Jewelry. At that time, although I had a lot of money in the bank, I still humbly took the job, but later regretted using a Master's degree to become a janitor. My job was to clean the ladies' and men's toilets and sweep the whole factory floor and dump garbage outside the building. I abhorred the job greatly because of some of the dirty women who never wrapped their bloodied menstrual pads, and I, as a dignified Ghanaian, was expected to collect them and throw them away. Also, the manager and the other people in the administration kept calling me "boy"- a rather derogatory name, just like "nigger."

I was beginning to feel proud and assert my Ghanaian male chauvinistic dignity. This later brought me headlong with my illness, for I was depressed about this sad state indeed. So, in June of 1983, I found myself at a psychiatric facility called Butler in Providence. Butler was the epitome of an excellent 'cuckoo's nest.' The grounds were a green mowed riot. Elm, conifers, apple trees decimated and punctuated the serene environment, provided shade and abundant oxygen. The rooms were fully air conditioned. There were basketball and tennis courts for the patients. There were always all kinds of delicious food in the refrigerator twenty-four hours a day and nurses changed the bed sheets every day and administered to the needs of the patients who didn't do much but sleep, play, and eat. There were statues and water fountains of colored bluish water everywhere. It was a real heaven for anyone to be there, and I loved it there tremendously. Could a lunatic enjoy such comfort? Well, only in civilized America. Our psychiatrists were the cream of the crop in America, as they came from Ivy League colleges like Brown University and Harvard. I always got care from the best doctors. I got very good care and was out of there in two weeks.

When I was discharged, I asked myself, "Why sit in America with a Master's degree working as a janitor and spending foolishly all my saved hard-earned dollars? What if I run out of money? Why not take this money and start an altogether new life in Ghana, find a girl who will love me, and marry and start a family?" My questions seemed valid so on November 11, 1983, despite the fact that I knew Ghana was facing severe drought and famine and receiving the economic brunt from the expulsion of about a million Ghanaians from Nigeria, I bought a ticket, packed a few things in four suitcases, and off I was on a Ghana-bound KLM Airline. It was a daredevil decision, for I didn't know what lay in wait for me politically, economically, and employment-wise. I had been in the U.S. for almost a decade. We passed through Amsterdam and Lagos, and finally, at about 8:30 P.M., we were in Accra, the Ghanaian capital. I had written to no one, so nobody met me at the airport. I took a taxi and got to Adehye Hotel with the help of a kind taxi driver, and slept overnight before traveling to Kumasi on a government transport bus.

Everybody, including my mother and brother and sisters were astonished to see me come home all the way from America unannounced, and with only four suitcases after a ten-year stay.

"Where was the car? Where were the big refrigerator and deep freezer? Where was the money to buy, outright, a house?" they asked and kept asking me.

Their expectations were too high. However, I told them that I had a Master's degree and was coming to start work. They were very disappointed indeed.

During that time, Ghana was ruled by a rather young Jerry John Rawlings, a political upstart and usurper of constitutional political power, a political armed burglar who, together with Kojo Tsikata, ruled nepotically and at gun point. He courted Marxism, yet knew little about it, and he was the friend of the then international troublemaker, Colonel Muammar Al-Gaddaffi of Libya.

He ruled Ghana for more than twenty years after spilling the blood of Acheampong, Afrifa, and several others after a coup d'etat. After more than ten years of controversial leadership, he still had his eyes on the presidency and waited to rule on, quite typical of many African leaders who falsely and mistakenly think that African political power was created for them alone. Examples of such leaders are Kenneth Kaunda of Zambia, Eyadema of Togo, Houphouet Boigny of Ivory Coast, Kamuzu Banda of Malawi, Mobutu Sese Seko of Zaire, Dauda Jawara of Gambia, Kanyon Doe of Liberia, Siad Barre of Somalia, Mengistu Haille Mariam of Ethiopia, Samora Machel of Mozambique, Idi Amin Dada of Uganda, Hissene Habre of Niger, Omar Bongo of Gabon and Mugabe of Zimbabwe. Because of these arrogant leaders, Africa suffered, and continues to suffer untold hardships in the form of civil wars, total economic disintegration and collapse, political paranoia exhibited in the culture of silence and downright drought, famine, and starvation. Will someone advise these political dunces to leave mother Africa alone?

When I got to Kumasi, Ghana was under a dusk to dawn curfew. There was electricity rationing and not much food to go around. The same day I was in Kumasi, I met this wonderful girl whom her mother called "Mama" affectionately. She was slim, tall and shapely, and her lips were kissably pouty, trembling with kissing delight, and she had the decorous gait of a beauty queen. Was it God bringing us together? Today, I know it was God.

"Hello, who are you?" I spoke in English with a poignant and ever-recognizable American accent since every Ghanaian wants to identify with America. It was a plus for me.

"My name is Mama," she also said in crisp, correct English through a mellow and compassionate soprano.

"I've just returned from America, and I want to meet girls. My name is Kwame," I smiled mirthfully.

"Oh, really," she smiled delightfully.

"Where are you going?" I asked.

"I am going home."

"It is at Lobito, just ahead of us."

"Can I walk you home?"

"Sure, why not?"

"Thank you."

We crossed the street from the International Kumasi Sports Stadium, passed through Anwona Fanti New Town, and faced Lobito. When we arrived at the house, she told me it belonged to her aunt.

"My father died when I was very young, and my mother came to live in this one room with me and Pat, my sister. We used to live at St. Louis Secondary School Campus where my older sister was an English teacher, but now in Canada. We also used to live in Kentinkrono."

"Did you go to secondary school?"

"Oh, yes, my sister put me through St. Louis. I finished form five in 1982. Where did you go to secondary school?"

"St. Augustine's, Cape Coast."

"Yes, it's a very good school."

"Thank you. St. Louis is also a good girls' Catholic boarding school in Kumasi. I presume you were a boarder."

"Yes."

"Did you know that I am a graduate with a Master's degree?"

"Oh, I always dream of marrying a graduate!"

"Well, you are seeing one now!"

"Are you already hinting at marriage? We just met," she said and smiled, and wished she had never said it.

"Why not?"

"I am too young."

"How old are you?"

"Just twenty."

"That's not young. I am twenty-nine."

"Oh."

"We can really be a fine couple someday."

As we talked, her mother approached.

"Hello. Mama, who is this man?"

"He is a new friend from America. We just met, and he is already talking about marriage."

"You must be lucky. A real American? Thank God and count your blessings," she said.

She smiled and Mama and I smiled too. We continued talking for a while, and as it was getting to curfew time, I had to hurry back to my mother's house at New Amakom.

"I'll have to go."

I gave Mama a thousand cedis, much to her surprise and delight and told her I would be back the following day in the afternoon.

"Bye-bye," she said with a radiant smile.

"Bye."

I ran home as it was almost 6 P.M., the time of the stupid curfew. Uneducated soldiers marshaled us like we were animals ready to be controlled and manipulated because they had guns. When I got home, my mother and brothers and sisters were indoors. I had supper and talked for a while before I retired to the hall to sleep on a mat on the floor.

The next day, I went job searching. I had already applied to be in the Foreign Service in Ghana while I was in Rhode Island. However, when I took the test, some Ewe sixth formers were taken instead, while I, a Master's degree holder and a Fanti, was rejected. So much for tribalism and nepotism. I didn't know where to turn, so the following Monday, I walked to T.I. Ahmadiyya Secondary School nearby, where Mr. Yusuf Effah, the headmaster, took me on the staff to teach English Literature and Biology in form five. He, of course, did so after inspecting my degrees and verifying my competence. I had not taught for a week, and my students took to me immediately. They called me "Ohio" and I patiently instructed them in Shakespeare's "Macbeth," Chaucer's "Pardoner's Tale," Ama Ata Aidoo's "Dilemma of a Ghost," and Jonathan Swift's "Gulliver's Travels."

The students were polite and well-dressed and morally disciplined. They called me "Sir."

The school administration gave me a nice, cozy bungalow two miles away from school. I walked back and forth to school every day. I furnished the two bedroom apartment and invited my senior brother to leave my mother's two-room tenement to come and live with me. He was more than happy to do so and live at Asokwa because it was a good neighborhood, and mostly for the rich and middle class in Kumasi.

One day, I invited Mama over when I had known and dated her for a while (I had had to adjust my dosage of Haloperidol so that I was strong and potent, full of sexual ammunition and rearmament). I was able to do it, and do it with gusto too, considering all that I had learned from Valencia. She said I was the first to mingle my juices with her jism and succeeded in letting her have a thunderous orgasm. I felt full of machismo and pride.

I was eager to take Mama formally as my wife. So I said to her one evening when she visited, "Mama, do you like me?"

"Well, yes."

"Do you like me a lot?"

"Kwame, I wouldn't be with you if I didn't like you."

"So you might say you love me."

"Sure, very much. You are a good guy."

"Thank you. It happens that I love you very much too."

"Let's get married then."

"Oh, you took the words out of my mouth."

"Good. You can perform the customary and traditional marital rites and pay the bride price to my relatives."

I was running out of money, therefore, I wrote to my American father and Dr. and Mrs. Halvorson. My dad sent me 500 dollars, and unexpectedly and surprisingly, I got 400 dollars from the Halvorsons. I didn't hesitate at all, so I bought the liquor, got my uncle and mother together, and with a few friends went to Mama's uncle's house at Ashanti New Town to effect the formalizing of the marriage traditionally. After my uncle set the ball rolling, he offered the liquor to Mama's uncle and relatives. Mama's uncle asked for the bride price and I gave forty thousand credis. I loved Mama so I made the dowry quite big.

Before then, Mama had been asked if she truly wanted me to be her husband to love and cherish me. Mama said, "Yes." I was the happiest man in the world. Mama's uncle offered everybody beer for refreshment. We took it after tons and tons of advice of do's and don'ts in a marriage. After the ceremony, we were husband and wife. There was no Western wedding in a church or court or anything, but our traditional marriage was recognized by all.

Mama moved to my bungalow and we started our happy marriage, not devoid of big problems brought about by my psychosis, but later resolved by the grace of God. Finally, Kwame had a winner to love him. Thank God. Soon Mama was pregnant with a child. On June 7, 1985, she gave birth to a bouncing baby boy.

Damn Mephistopheles and the other devils and demons too were working hard, and succeeded in jolting me with psychosis two weeks after my baby was born. It was a really difficult time for my wife, too young to understand what was happening to me. All the time, even in my preoccupation with my psychosis, I prayed that God give her immense courage to battle this novel and hard-to-take state of affairs for anyone especially, a young one like her, in a country where the mentally sick are looked upon with much derision.

Mental illness and psychiatry in Africa and Ghana is cruel as well as it is brutal. I was sent to Accra psychiatric hospital where, immediately, I was given a very painful injection of the hypnotic drug Paraldehyde. The reason why I said psychiatry is cruel is that the nurse who administered the injection deliberately manipulated the injection to cause a lot of pain. Immediately when he took out the needle, my butt was swollen and I couldn't walk. I later walked with a limp for about two weeks. No one reprimanded the nurse.

At that time, there was the rampant incidences of psychosis in young adults brought about by the smoking of wee or cannabis or marijuana in the country. The psychiatrist, Dr. Asare, thinking that I had been smoking wee, put me in Special Ward. And, Special Ward was living hell. It was the ultimate in filth. There were open receptacles of defecation. There was no toilet paper. Most of the patients walked around naked, displaying fat phalluses and were among the most aggressive patients. In my state, I called myself sane when I compared myself to these tough and deranged guys. Most of them were criminally insane, always involved in dangerous fights. One night someone bit off the nose of a patient. Another two almost blinded a patient. We slept on wooden planks as old as the hospital itself and infested with bed bugs and body lice. After I slept there one night in a lot of pain, I was covered, all over the body, with big body lice. I was praying hard that Mama wouldn't come to Accra to find me in that state, which would make her say "good-bye" and call it quits. Today, I marvel at the wonders and miracles of God for He sent Mama to Special Ward and she cried seeing me in that state.

It happened that she had received a letter from my American father bearing a check for two hundred dollars. Mama needed me to sign the check. I gladly signed it for her and she sympathetically cheered me up. She was great and courageous. When she was leaving, she cried, held my hand, and said she loved me very much and that she was chosen by God to take care of me. I couldn't help it and my eyes were blurred with unshed tears. Pretty soon they were streaming down my cheeks. My wife wiped them with her handkerchief and she left after saying that my son was with his grandmother and doing well.

The country then was in a harsh and dire economic condition, so the food in the hospital was not fit for an African dog. We had a small ladleful of gruel made from yellow corn that the United States was sending us as aid because of our drought. The porridge didn't have sugar in it, and sometimes there were worms and insect larvae in it. When I found that I just didn't eat and just pretended to be fasting. I prayed a lot. I knew what yellow corn was used for in the United States. It was given to swine and cattle to fatten them before butchering. I didn't understand why the U. S. didn't send us hamburgers, steak, hotdogs and sausages. Maybe, they thought Africans didn't deserve the best.

In the afternoon, for lunch, we were given two small ladles of gari and a half ladle of beans whose palm oil had been deliberately taken away by the nurses. It was very dangerous to eat the gari with such little beans for fear of being choked; and you guessed it, there was no drinking water in the ward. It was just done intentionally to punish the patients whose only fault was that they were unfortunate enough to fall sick. Being new to the place, and always comparing it to Butler in Providence in the United States, I once almost died because I didn't know how to eat the food, and I was choking and breathless. There was nobody to do the Heimlich maneuver on me and with difficulty, I was literally dying. After trying to cough to expel the choking lump from my throat, God saved me by letting me cough the lump up after about a two-minute bout with coughing and choking. It is a well-known fact that if a person is out of breath for four minutes, it is his deathbed. I thanked God and abandoned the food. I was losing weight rapidly. Later, I learned how to eat the gari. I would eat the little beans first and eat the gari in tiny morsels. A whole meal of that little plate took me about two hours to finish.

In the evening, we were given a lump of yellow corn Ga kenkey and a little bit of ground red pepper without tomatoes. Prisoners would not even be treated like that. What has the mentally sick done to be subjected to this dehumanizing inhumanity? God created a mentally sick person too, you know, and maybe there is a strange connection between high intelligence, creativity and mental illness, for Hemingway, Lord Byron, Emily Dickinson, Dostoevsky, Nietzsche, and Van Gogh had problems like this.

We were ordered inside immediately after supper and we didn't come out until the next morning at nine, when the door was opened for us to go for our wormy pap without sugar or bread. In the meantime, there were fights.

What bothered me most was the morning during medication. There was only one cup and a bucket of water and the nurse would give an arbitrary dose of Melleril, sometimes a too large dosage of the drug which had serious side effects to a patient. The other patients were filthy with rank and acid morning unbrushed and stinking mouths, and I just couldn't drink from the same cup with them, so I chewed my medication, no matter how malicious the taste was. This was the condition and dire situation at Special Ward, quite unfit a place, the habitat of schizophrenics, manic depressives, alcoholics, and drug psychotics. It was a really tough place, and anyone who passed through this ward is a really tough person indeed, only receiving his strength from the good Lord.

One thing that bothered me a lot in Ghana was, of all the ten years I had been in the country and at the hospital, not once did the doctor send me for blood work. Therefore, if a patient's kidney or liver were atrophying or not due to the side effects of the medication, no one cared- at least, not in a third world country. It was in this situation that I appreciated St. Peter State Hospital, Upham Hall and Butler. Of course, there is not even the least comparison between a third world country and a first world like the great United States of America.

Chapter XVII

Back to the Ahmadiyya Secondary School, and Redundancy and Back to America, 1992

The very bad conditions and treatment at the hospital in Accra made every patient try very hard to get better quickly and leave the awful pleace. Surprisingly, that cruel way of treating African lunatics worked; for, in no time, I was getting aware of my sane self. When I had completely recuperated, I was discharged. Mama came all the way from Kumasi to get me. She burned all my clothes due to the lice.

I returned to Kumasi and went back to T.I. Ahmadiyya Secondary School to report back and teach. The headmaster surprisingly told me that I was redundant and couldn't teach anymore. I knew it was because my personality had been tainted by a bout of psychosis. I didn't know what to do. What bothered me most was that if I was out of T.I. Ahmadiyya, the authorities were definitely going to evict me from my bungalow and I wouldn't have a place to stay. Already, the assistant headmaster, Mrs. Ntiforo, had given me two weeks to quit the bungalow. I had only a couple of weeks to try and find a school and a place to live.

Immediately, I traveled to Accra Post Office, the only place one could make an international call at that time in Ghana, where I made a three minute call to my American father, Mr. Aga, in the United States. He said he would wire me money immediately through the Barclays Bank in Ghana. I went to most of the schools in Kumasi including Opoku Ware, Prempeh,

Anglican Secondary School, Kumasi High School, Yaa Asantewaa and St. Louis Secondary, but I was always given the same answer, "No opening."

I then had to go to the rural areas (places where no teacher wanted to stay because of lack of amenities like electricity and good drinking water) and to outlying small villages to try to secure a teaching position in a village secondary school. I went to Atwimaman Secondary School at Trabuom, whose headmaster was a white naturalized Ghanaian from Britain. I told him I could teach biology, general science, English language and literature, French, Latin, or Greek.

"I am sorry, but there is no opening," he said, "Thank you for coming to our school to apply," he continued.

I was running out of time.

"Why don't you try at Ejisu Secondary School twelve miles away from Kumasi?" Mama told me, quite concerned indeed. I had to work to shelter and feed the small family. My wife had given birth to a baby girl at that time, so I had two mouths and a wife to feed. I went to Ejisu the next day. The headmaster of the secondary school was not sure about taking me onto his staff, so with a lot of excuses and procrastination, he asked me to come again and again. After going there for the sixth time, he said he could employ me but asked, "Why do you want to leave a good secondary school in the city of Kumasi where there is everything like electricity, sports stadium for soccer matches, good drinking water, and the biggest open market in West Africa to come to a desolate place like here to teach?"

I just couldn't give him an answer. I stood quietly and let an ugly silent minute elapse. Then he said, "I'll contact your former headmaster to find out if you are a good man and a teacher."

"Okay, sir. You can," I said sadly.

It happened that as I was away for almost a couple of weeks, my students at T.I. Ahmadiyya Secondary School, considering my teaching ability and sound academic competence, were pestering the headmaster to bring me back to continue to teach them. They said they wanted no one but me. The headmaster, under considerable pressure from the students, agreed to bring me back and sent for me. I got there the following morning and was told to go to class. That was the end of my debacle. I prayed to thank God because he restored me and had only tested me without necessarily taking away my job and bungalow.

I taught the kids until they took the G.C.E. examination. They all did well with one person getting I, three people getting 2, and several others getting 3s. No one failed the exam. I was very happy that, at least, even I could help shape kids' minds to help them in the future. I continued to teach and taught on for ten consecutive years until 1992 in January when I had another relapse of the illness. In all the nine years, my American father kept up correspondence with me, sending me a two hundred dollar check at the end of every couple of months.

Mama was a Catholic like myself, but as she contemplated the activities of some priests who molested altar boys and had rampant sex with women and acted foolishly and were bent on almost destroying the church, she made a bold decision and left the Catholic church to join a Pentecostal evangelistic church- The Church of Pentecost at the Asokwa McKwoen Temple. I was disappointed that she didn't have enough faith to remain a Catholic despite its shortcomings, and I attended church service at the Old Asokwa St. Francis of Assisi Catholic Church.

I will spare the reader the details about what I went through again at the Accra hospital when I was put there because it was rather awful. I was subjected to cruel beatings by nurses and locked up in a water-laden, rat-infested cell for a couple of days. They sometimes even forgot to bring me food and water. This was at overcrowded Ward E. What I suffered badly in the cell in Ward E was unbearable thirst as you know that I was taking Lithium and was always thirsty.

A nightmare of faithless self-doubt haunted me, and Mama and myself were really sad and prayed hard and fasted. Somebody told Mama about a powerful evangelistic charismatic church at Ohwim, Kumasi where it was believed there were miraculous healings and expulsion of demons from people with difficult problems.

Mama took me there after she herself had been there praying and fasting on account of me. When I saw the reverend in charge, he immediately prayed a powerfully long and fervid prayer and blessed me. He asked me to do a three consecutive day dry fasting.

I did the fasting and prayed, and would you believe that on the final day of my fasting, I went to my mailbox at Ahmadiyya and found a letter from my first American brother, Tom Salt. It was a letter honoring me to come to the United States and come back to Alexandria, Minnesota, to give a speech at our 20th anniversary reunion of our high school graduation.

God's wonders will never end. I had even not corresponded with Tom (chairman of the reunion organizing committee) for almost twenty years, but he remembered me and my American Field Service days with him and invited me. I took the letter to the American Consulate in the American Embassy in Accra. In less than ten minutes, the consul gave me a visa. Imagine that! Because an American visa in Africa is like a treasure of gold.

My two brothers helped and bought me a plane ticket and gave me a one thousand dollars, and on July 1, 1992, in the evening, I boarded a British Airways plane that flew through Kano, Nigeria, and London and to New York's Kennedy Airport. I was definitely glad to be in the United States for the fourth time. I took a Northwest Airline, which charged me a staggering four hundred dollars, and arrived in Minneapolis at 8:30 Minneapolis time. As I knew Minnesota well, I took a taxi to the Greyhound bus station and waited until 2:30 A.M., all worn out, and took the bus to Alexandria.

I arrived at Alexandria at 6:30 A.M. I called my American father, Mr. Aga, whose voice I was delighted to hear. He came for me at the bus station. There was a three-week interval before the reunion, so Tom invited me to stay with him and his mother Mrs. Salt, who had undergone surgery on both knees and had been in a scary ten day coma. Mrs. Salt was really glad to see me once again after almost twenty years, and gave me wonderful hospitality.

I prepared a speech and waited for July 25th for the reunion. It finally came and I gave a good speech, much to the admiration of my former classmates who were neurologists, pathologists, nurses, pilots, college professors, and publishers. Almost all of them were married with children. Roger was there, Paul was there, John was there, Riley was there, Margaret and Barb were there, and Nancy Bergstrom Anders was there too. We had a fantastic weekend full of celebration, belated conversation and good food and drinks.

My American father bought me a plane ticket to Rhode Island. I live in Pawtucket, Rhode Island and teach at Rhode Island College as an adjunct professor, and also work at Texas Instruments, and I am also the secretary of the Ghana Association of Rhode Island. I saved up all my money and built a $100,000 five bedroom house in Kotei, near Kumasi, and also bought a new Volvo S70. I had overcome these great odds and done something good for myself and family. For about eight years, I haven't relapsed. Definitely, I am overcoming manic depression as I grow older. Mania is full of extreme confidence, articulation and extreme energy and happiness, sometimes erotic, and hallucinatory. Anyone who has experienced two personalities-the normal and the "abnormal" without necessarily doing harm to himself or anyone is perhaps a living stoical sufferer.

I am always fascinated by the great state of Minnesota. It is this state that produced Hubert Humphrey, Walter Mondale and Ventura and Al Franken. It is also the state that produced Kofi Annan, the UN Secretary General (he went to Macalester College in St. Paul). It produced great writers like Sinclair Lewis and F. Scot Fitzgerald, and I am glad I was in Minnesota.

I always dream about the doctor I couldn't become when I was young. Maybe a research psychiatrist who would have worked extremely hard to help other mentally sick people.

My thirty five year journey with bipolar illness has humbled me and brought me closer to God and Jesus. They give me hope everyday. Even though uneducated people are ready to attribute shame and ridicule to the mentally sick, I have walked this world with tremendous achievements. Even if God calls me today, I will have no regrets at all.

Blessed be to God and all the people who have helped me. Indeed, God has done enough for me.

A television commercial always says "depression hurts." I say it doesn't hurt when you have the right people to help you. Depression is very treatable so if you encounter it, don't be ashamed. Seek help.

Printed in the United States
By Bookmasters